Martinique

WORLD BIBLIOGRAPHICAL SERIES

General Editors:
Robert G. Neville (Executive Editor)
John J. Horton

Robert A. Myers   Hans H. Wellisch
Ian Wallace   Ralph Lee Woodward, Jr.

John J. Horton is Deputy Librarian of the University of Bradford and currently Chairman of its Academic Board of Studies in Social Sciences. He has maintained a longstanding interest in the discipline of area studies and its associated bibliographical problems, with special reference to European Studies. In particular he has published in the field of Icelandic and of Yugoslav studies, including the two relevant volumes in the World Bibliographical Series.

Robert A. Myers is Associate Professor of Anthropology in the Division of Social Sciences and Director of Study Abroad Programs at Alfred University, Alfred, New York. He has studied post-colonial island nations of the Caribbean and has spent two years in Nigeria on a Fulbright Lectureship. His interests include international public health, historical anthropology and developing societies. In addition to *Amerindians of the Lesser Antilles: a bibliography* (1981), *A Resource Guide to Dominica, 1493-1986* (1987) and numerous articles, he has compiled the World Bibliographical Series volumes on *Dominica* (1987), *Nigeria* (1989) and *Ghana* (1991).

Ian Wallace is Professor of German at the University of Bath. A graduate of Oxford in French and German, he also studied in Tübingen, Heidelberg and Lausanne before taking teaching posts at universities in the USA, Scotland and England. He specializes in contemporary German affairs, especially literature and culture, on which he has published numerous articles and books. In 1979 he founded the journal *GDR Monitor*, which he continues to edit under its new title *German Monitor*.

Hans H. Wellisch is Professor emeritus at the College of Library and Information Services, University of Maryland. He was President of the American Society of Indexers and was a member of the International Federation for Documentation. He is the author of numerous articles and several books on indexing and abstracting, and has published *The Conversion of Scripts and Indexing and Abstracting: an International Bibliography*, and *Indexing from A to Z*. He also contributes frequently to *Journal of the American Society for Information Science*, *The Indexer* and other professional journals.

Ralph Lee Woodward, Jr. is Professor of History at Tulane University, New Orleans. He is the author of *Central America, a Nation Divided*, 2nd ed. (1985), as well as several monographs and more than seventy scholarly articles on modern Latin America. He has also compiled volumes in the World Bibliographical Series on *Belize* (1980), *El Salvador* (1988), *Guatemala* (Rev. Ed.) (1992) and *Nicaragua* (Rev. Ed.) (1994). Dr. Woodward edited the Central American section of the *Research Guide to Central America and the Caribbean* (1985) and is currently associate editor of Scribner's *Encyclopedia of Latin American History*.

VOLUME 175

Martinique

Janet Crane
Compiler

CLIO PRESS
OXFORD, ENGLAND · SANTA BARBARA, CALIFORNIA
DENVER, COLORADO

British Library Cataloguing in Publication Data

Martinique. – (World Bibliographical
series; vol. 175)
I. Crane, Janet   II. Series
016.972982

ISBN 1–85109–151–3

ABC-CLIO Ltd.,
Old Clarendon Ironworks,
35A Great Clarendon Street,
Oxford OX2 6AT, England.

───────────

ABC-CLIO Inc.,
130 Cremona Drive,
Santa Barbara,
CA 93116, USA.

Designed by Bernard Crossland
Typeset by Columns Design and Production Services Ltd, Reading, England.
Printed and bound in Great Britain by Bookcraft (Bath) Ltd., Midsomer Norton

THE WORLD BIBLIOGRAPHICAL SERIES

This series, which is principally designed for the English speaker, will eventually cover every country (and many of the world's principal regions), each in a separate volume comprising annotated entries on works dealing with its history, geography, economy and politics; and with its people, their culture, customs, religion and social organization. Attention will also be paid to current living conditions – housing, education, newspapers, clothing, etc.– that are all too often ignored in standard bibliographies; and to those particular aspects relevant to individual countries. Each volume seeks to achieve, by use of careful selectivity and critical assessment of the literature, an expression of the country and an appreciation of its nature and national aspirations, to guide the reader towards an understanding of its importance. The keynote of the series is to provide, in a uniform format, an interpretation of each country that will express its culture, its place in the world, and the qualities and background that make it unique. The views expressed in individual volumes, however, are not necessarily those of the publisher.

VOLUMES IN THE SERIES

For Riva

Contents

Contents

Introduction

Martinique is one of the Lesser Antilles, which on a world map resemble a tiny beaded necklace arched around the entrance to the Caribbean Sea, effectively separating it from the Atlantic Ocean to the east. Each island in the arc appears too small to distinguish individually and one could too easily assume that all share similar geological, biological, and cultural histories and features. To a certain degree this assumption is true, but once the student has acknowledged the commonalities and takes a closer look, each individual island is quite a world unto itself. It is with these attributes clearly in focus, shared origins with other islands in the chain and individual uniqueness, that Martinique is best approached. Part, indeed, of the fascination of Caribbean studies is determining how each island conforms to regional patterns but at the same time how its own history and geography are distinctive.

Politically and economically Martinique is an integral part of France, one of the country's four Overseas Departments, along with nearby Guadeloupe, also in the Lesser Antilles, Réunion, in the Indian Ocean, and French Guiana, on mainland South America. Indeed, Martinique has been French longer than some of the country's European metropolitan departments. In contrast to the independent former British Caribbean colonies, Martinique each year becomes ever more dependent on the metropolis and isolated politically and economically from its nearby Caribbean neighbours, with whom it has far more in common.

Some of Martinique's uniqueness and enigma, then, stem from this umbilical cord to France, nurtured over the decades by the French policy of assimilation. There has been a conscious educational, political, and cultural effort to have the colony's (and now, the department's) identity stem from the mother country, with the result that migration, travel, goods, ideas, and money flow largely between France and Martinique. Ideally, the Martinican imagines herself to be *française*, with all the metropolitan values and associations that implies, and with France the solution to the island's economic dilemmas. Pierre-Laval Sainte-Rose's work has shown that the overwhelming majority of Martinican young people now expect to go to France to study, work, or learn a trade, and many permanently.

In reality, most Martinicans are poor and their history, ethnicity, and life-styles are unmistakably Caribbean. The island's population consists largely of mixed European and African ancestry; its everyday language is a French-based creole which is virtually unintelligible to a metropolitan Frenchwoman; and its culture is rich with elements not only from France, but also from Africa and the long-vanished Amerindian populations who once inhabited the island. These are attributes Martinique also shares with its Caribbean neighbours.

The geophysical environment

Martinique is the largest of the Lesser Antilles. With 425 square miles, it is more than ten times the size of the much smaller Montserrat, a northern island in the arc, and twice that of St. Lucia, its nearest neighbour to the south. Volcanic in origin, it continues to be formed and modified by modern-day eruptions.

The entire Caribbean rim is a geophysically active region, with the relatively small Caribbean tectonic plate being squeezed on the west by the Cocos Plate and on the east by the Atlantic Plate. The Lesser Antilles chain is an island arc formed by the head-on collision of the westward-moving North American Plate and the much smaller Caribbean Plate. Such arcs are formed where lighter submerged edges of continental plates ride up as heavier oceanic plates are subducted down into the molten core (other examples being the Aleutians, the Ryukyus, and the Marianas). Volcanic activity is stimulated deep within the crust, and all of the high Antilles were formed this way, although only St. Vincent and Martinique are presently considered volcanically active.

The volcanic islands comprise the inner arc of two parallel groups of islands; this inner arc is composed of high islands with one or more volcanic craters. The islands of the outer arc, which include Barbados, Barbuda, and Grande Terre, are by contrast low and coralline in nature, primarily of limestone. This difference in origins and the varying ages of volcanic islands contributes to the great diversity of Antillean geological environments.

Mont Pelée, which looms over northern Martinique, reaches 1,400 metres and is the third highest point in the Lesser Antilles. It erupted twice in 1902 and its vent produced a series of eruptions in 1929-32.

These eruptions were among the most observed of the modern era, and volcanologists have since named *nuées ardentes*, the explosive gaseous eruptions accompanied by exceedingly high temperatures and abundant pyroclastic material, after Mont Pelée, referring to them as Pelean-style eruptions.

The northern two-thirds of Martinique are largely composed of geologically recent lava flows from Pelée and previously active vents, which have resulted in the extensive interior highlands there. The southern third of the island is much lower in elevation, composed of the hilly, more eroded material from earlier volcanic activity. Vulcanism, earthquakes, and fumarole activity are common on Martinique and, indeed, are likely to occur anywhere along the Lesser Antillean subduction zone on which the island is located.

The Baie of Fort-de-France is a large, deep, and protected natural harbour on Martinique's Caribbean coast, around which the island virtually appears to curl. The extensive coastal plain there on which the capital city now sits, gives way to a large amphitheatre-like valley into which rivers that drain the highlands flow. By contrast, the Atlantic Coastal plain is narrower and its slopes are shorter and steeper.

Climate and biota

Martinique is the northernmost of the Windward Islands, by which name the southern half of the Lesser Antilles arc is known. The island lies in the belt of westward-moving trade winds and this, in addition to its relatively high elevations, gives the island a great variety of microenvironments. The windward northeast coast receives abundant rainfall, in places well over 250 centimetres a year, whereas the leeward and more protected west coast is far drier, even susceptible to drought. Short streams, arising in the wet interior highlands, flow down slopes across the island landscape. It is where they meet the sea that most settlements are located.

Temperatures are mild everywhere because of the trade winds, and average annual temperature ranges are less than three degrees centigrade. Many coastal residents nonetheless maintain second homes in the northern highlands because of even milder conditions there. In general, however, the southern and western sections of the island are drier and sunnier, and therefore have greater temperature variations.

Martinique lies directly in the path of warm equatorial counter currents, so that offshore waters are year-round about twenty-seven degrees centigrade. Oceanic currents usually follow surface winds and the island therefore sits in the extreme hurricane belt; between August and October it is highly susceptible to damaging storms. In the last thirty years, three major hurricanes have devastated the island, the most recent in August of 1993.

The highlands in northern and central Martinique support a luxuriant montane tropical rainforest. Its structure is true rainforest and many trees are supported by buttresses and stilt roots. Few branches grow from lower trunks, but a tuft of leaves appears perhaps twenty to thirty metres up to form the crown of taller trees. The forest is evergreen, with individual trees shedding their leaves gradually and throughout the year. These mixed evergreen forests contain towering individuals of such genera as *Calophyllum, Cedrela, Ceiba, Chrysophyllum, Genipa, Guarea, Lucuma, Pithecelobium, Sloanea, Sterculia,* and *Swietenia*, all well-known components of neotropical rainforests, as well as *Dussia*, a genus found only in the Antilles.

Martinique's native flora also displays the characteristics that make island biotas everywhere so valuable and fascinating. There is a high degree of endemism – species and subspecies found nowhere else; adaptive radiation of related forms from a single ancestral species, and arborescence (particularly in evidence among the abundant tree-ferns on the island). Delicate *Euterpe* palms, shrubby aralias (*Clusia* spp.), and tree-ferns occur both in these mixed forests and in more specialized, single-species stands on the highest, exposed slopes.

Trees support many unique species of vines, bromeliads, orchids, and other epiphytes on their upper branches and the numerous species of mosses and ferns distinguish the understorey of humid Martinican forests. Many epiphytes and species of the forest floor have become well-known as house plants in American and European homes. Overall, a sort of tiered canopy of vegetation occurs in these rainforests – one that allows plants to take full advantage of varying light, humidity, and growing surfaces, from the crowns of trees to dead trunks on the forest floor.

Southern forests, by contrast, are deciduous and often scrubby, with the spines, protective hairs and leathery skins that make this vegetation adapted to frequent drought and brush fires. Although indigenous trees such as *Tabebuia* (Antillean pears), *Malphigia* (wild cherries), and *Zanthoxylum* (nut-trees) still survive in small remnant stands, this is an impoverished vegetation. Martinique's strand or beach species tend to be those that are widespread throughout the Caribbean and which are salt tolerant and carried by currents. Mammey apples (*Mammea americana*), caimito (*Chrysophyllum cainito*), manchineel (*Hippomane mancinella*), and sea grape (*Coccoloba uvifera*) are numerous, as are more cosmopolitan introduced species like coconut (*Cocus nucifera*) and bamboos (*Bambusa* spp.). In addition, the island still has sizeable areas of coastal mangroves.

Natural vegetation on Martinique has largely been altered by humans and animals not native to the island, so that in many areas introduced exotics have totally displaced, or now mingle with, indigenous species. Recent volcanic eruptions, too, have destroyed mature mixed forests and often create conditions favourable to secondary species or single species stands. *Cecropia*, a distinctive and widespread neotropical genus, is visible everywhere on disturbed sites. Strong winds at higher elevations and geothermal activity are associated with specialized vegetation such as terrestrial orchids and elfin woodlands.

There are fewer forested acres per capita on Martinique than on most of the other islands of the Lesser Antilles, a reflection on the island's extremely high population density. What public forest remains, about 8,000 hectares largely in the Pelée region, is protected and therefore fairly stable. The rest of the island bears the heavy imprint of human activity and small dooryard and market gardens dot the Martinican landscape. Commercial crops have been planted wherever slopes will permit; on the wetter east coast and lower slopes of Pelée, this means banana trees whilst on the drier western and southern slopes sugarcane is still the predominant crop, as it has been since the late 17th century.

All over the island, the ornamental fruit and shade trees, as well as most garden flowers, are introduced tropical and subtropical species from Asia, Africa, and mainland South America. A small number of these plants have become so widely distributed that today yards and public places have a remarkable similarity throughout the tropical world. Clarissa Kimber has recently written a superb monograph on Martinique's vegetative history, which includes numerous regional maps as well as detailed diagrams of individual food and ornamental gardens. Richard Howard's monumental work on Antillean plants is the source to consult for identification, distribution, and other basic attributes of Martinique's flora.

Native fauna has suffered over the last 500 years, for a variety of reasons. After the European invasion, more forests were cleared for plantations, reducing the natural habitat. Eurasian farm animals were introduced along with cosmopolitan pests like rats and mongooses, which carried diseases and crowded out specialized natives. Hunting also exerted an increased pressure on all species since, regardless of Amerindian numbers before the invasion, after the introduction of slave labour in the 18th century the human population on the islands was significantly increased. Birds of all types were assiduously hunted and their populations dramatically reduced. However, although for many years several subspecies unique to the island were thought to have disappeared, known extinctions now appear to be few.

Native mammals are few in number and include several species of bats and the *agouti* (*Dasyprocta*), which appears to have flourished everywhere in the Americas alongside humans. Martinique is also home to two species of *fer-de-lance*, the much-feared poisonous relatives of rattlesnakes, which are found throughout the American tropics. While there are numerous field guides on Caribbean birds, butterflies, and reeflife, all of which can be used on Martinique, there are no studies on Martinique's terrestrial fauna.

Today's landscape on Martinique is one that largely reflects intensive human activities during the last 2,000 years, and that includes abundant representatives from a vigorous exchange of species with Africa and Asia. Most flora that the visitor will observe at elevations below about 300 metres is either introduced or composed of widely-distributed American species. It is only at higher elevations in more secluded sites that there are small reserves for indigenous species with limited distributions. There is a pressing need for a systematic survey of Martinican flora and fauna.

Prehistory and archaeology

The earliest human beings on Martinique most likely came from northern South America and Trinidad, at least 2,100 years ago, and archaeological sites bearing radiocarbon dates of circa 1,800 years before the present (BP) are relatively common on the island. These sites are associated with peoples of the Saladoid ceramic-making tradition, who have been linked with Arawakan-speaking peoples. Early settlements were concentrated near the sea on the windward coast, located at upland sites along freshwater streams. Faunal analysis of such sites shows inhabitants relying on a diverse diet of fish and other aquatic animals, birds, and terrestrial animals. The dietary staple was bitter manioc. Although no population estimates have been attempted, a flourishing population was apparently devastated at least once by an eruption of Mont Pelée, for there are long gaps in the archaeological record at some sites that correspond to periods when volcanic materials changed dramatically. M. J. Roobol, H. Petitjean-Roget and A. L. Smith have speculated on this important link between human settlement, population numbers and location, and volcanic activity. Their work, and that of Mario Mattioni, has contributed to recognition of the likely impact of volcanic eruptions on prehistoric human settlements and their continuity on the island. Later settlements, whose sites on Martinique occur from 1,550 years ago to 500 years ago, employed increasingly plain and rudimentary ceramic techniques. Engraving and incising, which were abundant in sites 1,750 years ago, became rarer by 1550 BP, and completely disappeared at some sites by 1,000 years ago. It was this gradual decline in ceramic sophistication, and an increased orientation to the sea, evident in shellfish remains, that led archaeologists to postulate Carib migrations to the Antilles around 1,000 years ago, with their displacement of Arawakans in the Lesser Antilles ongoing at the time of European contact. However, this theory is no longer accepted, and the fieldwork and new interpretations by Louis Allaire and Mario Mattioni, originally conducted on Martinique in the 1960s and 1970s, have been vital to this reorientation in Antillean prehistory. Mattioni proposed that individual groups of people moved regularly, and that this would conceivably result in stratigraphic aberrations in the archaeological record. Martinique, indeed, is among the richest of the Lesser Antillean islands in its prehistoric sites, with many represented by three or more distinct horizons over an 800-year period.

Archaeological study on Martinique owes its beginnings to a civil servant, Eugéne Revert, and a Catholic father, Robert Pinchon, who excavated island sites in the late 1930s and the 1940s; the many early publications of Pinchon and Henri and Jacques Petitjean-Roget attest to the great number of Martinican sites and their horizontal depth and diversity. Preceramic sites have also been described for Martinique, but dates and associations of these peoples are still unclear.

Most archaeological complexes are on the north and east coasts, with numerous separate contemporaneous sites adjacent to almost every small stream that empties into the Atlantic Ocean. These early Saladoid peoples most likely moved into the Lesser Antilles, throughout which they were widespread, from Venezuela and Trinidad approximately 2,100 years ago. Over the next 1,500 years, perhaps due to isolation from more innovative and advanced potters on the continent, ceramic techniques degenerated and sites reveal a stronger reliance on lambi (*Strombus gigas*) and other sea foods, instead of an agricultural and terrestrially-oriented faunal diet. The picture emerges of a well-inhabited island for most of the last twenty-one hundred years, with individual settlement sites, particularly in the northern part of the island, being dramatically affected by volcanic eruptions and other environmental factors over the centuries. The paper by Irving Rouse and Allaire is the best available summary of both a regional and Martinican prehistory.

For all of these pre-Columbian pottery-making peoples the staple of the diet was cassava (*Manihot utilissima*). Cassava is a root crop domesticated in tropical South America that thrives in well-drained, mineral-poor soils; it is among the most efficient starch-producing plants known, with both sweet and bitter varieties. In the latter, poisonous prussic acid must be removed by an elaborate pressing process that leaves a coarse, storable meal. The wide-mouthed pots into which juice was dripped and the large platters on which flour was cooked and dried, characterize Arawakan archaeological sites on Martinique and throughout most of eastern South America and the Caribbean.

The sweet variety of cassava was one of many less important root crops, such as sweet potatoes and several aroids, which were eaten boiled. All are of probable South American origins. Maize, too, was grown on Martinique, with its Middle American accompaniments of beans and squash – although the South American cultigens were by far the most important, reflecting the cultural associations of the people. The diet, agricultural techniques, settlement patterns, and languages of Martinique's aboriginal peoples all show closer affinities to the peoples of northern and Amazonian South America than to those of Central America. This relationship has generated the now widely-accepted theory that prehistoric peopling of the West Indies proceeded from the south and not from either the north or west.

Historical Period

Not much is known of the Amerindian populations on Martinique between 1493 and 1635, the earliest years of European disruption. We are fortunate to have the excellent and now classic accounts from the Dominican friars Jean-Baptiste DuTertre and R. P. Labat for the 17th century. Both had extensive contacts with native inhabitants, and described their way of life as well as their interactions with the new occupants of the island.

The peoples encountered by the Europeans were Caribs, and not Arawaks, the displacement of whom has still not been satisfactorily explained. Caribs, while horticulturalists, were far more oriented to the sea and hunting than their Arawakan predecessors. At the time of European contact, they were apparently actively expanding their territory from northern South America.

The first permanent European settlements on Martinique were established in 1635 by the French, and the island has been under virtual French control, with one short interruption, ever since. Early colonists were sent from France under the auspices of various commercial ventures, with indigo, cotton, tobacco, and coffee among the first successful cash crops. It was long accepted that until sugarcane was established in the later years of the 17th century, colonists experimented in vain for a lucrative commodity. In truth, it now seems clear that the colony prospered from the very beginning, or at least the French landowners and Dutch merchants did relatively well. Instead, it was the French crown that struggled with various arrangements for many years to increase its own proportion of and control over the new wealth emanating from its American island colonies. See the excellent studies by Philip Boucher and Nellis Crouse on early European settlements on Martinique.

It was Colbert, Louis XIV's Minister of Finance from 1661 to 1683, who drew up the locally-abhorred *exclusif*, a mercantilist policy whereby Martinican planters were obliged to deal only with French ships and traders, who could then dictate markets to colonists. From its earliest days Martinique had an active triangular trade that involved New Orleans, and another with New England. The island also became the centre of New World French privateering, the lucrative business of illegal trading and preying upon the commercial ships of other colonial powers. Thanks to their opportunism on all fronts, the free islanders thrived, but by the early years of the 18th century the island's future became linked to sugarcane, slavery, and a small number of large estate owners. The crown was never able to rigorously enforce the *exclusif*.

So prosperous were Martinique and Guadeloupe that, when France lost her holdings in North America, the much-reduced empire that centred on these islands was still considered a lucrative and substantial one. Most of France's colonial policies in the late 18th and throughout the 19th century were written specifically for these sugar islands.

Many French merchants, and Martinicans as well, prospered because of the slave trade. Martinique served the regrettable role of being a major slave entrepôt, as ships bound for Saint Dominique (later Haiti), New Orleans, and Guadeloupe regularly stopped there first and slaves were sold and often resold. Robert Stein has written a valuable general history of French slaving.

The French slave trade was abolished after 1814, but slavery persisted in Martinique until 1848, some seventeen years longer than in the British Caribbean. The end of slavery was finally brought about by metropolitan politics which were heavily influenced by British liberals. The vicissitudes of the official French experience with slavery are confusing; moreover, local laws and practice on Martinique often conflicted with French policy, and such metropolitan policy occasioned several serious political uprisings on the island. Slave emancipation was first effected and lasted for eight short years during the Republic in the 1790s; then slavery was reinstituted with the monarchy. Seymour Drescher and David Geggus have written about aspects of the French slave emancipation laws and the reaction by white politicians and slaves on Martinique.

The overwhelming consensus seems to be that bad as conditions for slaves were on the French islands, they were even worse in the English colonies. The role of the Roman Catholic church and its missionaries, as well as the widespread miscegenation between French masters and their slave women, who were frequently freed and given property, are often credited for this difference. Slave life in the French American colonies, both *en route* and in island milieus, has recently prompted wide attention in academic studies, although this literature is nonetheless still quite meagre. The descriptive work of Gabriel Debien on Martinican slaves, based on French archival sources and published entirely in French, deserves mention here. The more recent studies of Dale Tomich have tied slavery and slave conditions to planter economic strategies and global economics, but much about slave life remains to be disclosed.

Most slaves were given rights to provisioning grounds, small plots of land on which they could grow food crops, as well as some time during the week to cultivate them. Despite the continuing importation of foods from abroad, by the mid-19th century most of Martinique's food needs were being produced on these plots by slaves, an arrangement that lowered planter costs. When emancipation was effected, planters accepted the rights of former slaves to these lands and the basis for family smallholdings was established. Maroons, runaway slaves, occupied and cultivated lands in the less accessible interior highlands; these lands, too, have remained with their descendants. Maroons, with their independent spirit and resiliency, have provided a symbol of hope for Martinican writer Edouard Glissant, who contrasts them with the more dependent, easily satisfied slaves of the lowlands.

When Martinique's slaves were emancipated the French had to look elsewhere for a labour supply, largely turning to Tamil-speaking indentured labourers from southern India. As many as 25,000 were brought to Martinique in the late 1800s, but most eventually returned to their homeland, with those who stayed intermarrying with the Afro-Caribbean population. Their influence is still visible in the Martinican landscape and culture as small Hindu temples, a syncretistic element in all aspects of island folk religion, and a few Tamil-based words in island Creole.

Almost no literature exists in English, or in French for that matter, on the period between Emancipation in 1848 and Departmentalization one hundred years later. This means a reliance on travellers' accounts, which too frequently are romanticized and superficial. Two noteworthy exceptions are the classic accounts of Martinique by Lafcadio Hearn and George Kennan, both among the most peripatetic and prolific of Victorian travellers. Their writings remain as fresh and charming as when they were penned.

Historical studies on Martinique have tended to focus on Europeans, the relationship of the island to France, and on political and economic activities. Studies reflect not only the white, European interests but their perspective as well. Plantation society in Martinique, however, was composed of *Békés* or white creoles, an extremely small, endogamous group of island-born whites; a slightly larger, but important group of freed persons of colour, many of whom became tradesmen, shop owners, fisherfolk, and small farmers in the interior hill country; and the overwhelming majority in the society, slaves. The literature available is virtually in inverse proportion to the group's numerical representation.

Contemporary Martinique

In 1946 Martinicans, led by their most prominent political representative, Aimé Césaire, voted overwhelmingly to become a French Overseas Department instead of gaining independence This decision appears to have been decisive for Martinique's subsequent evolution into what many have termed a French-subsidized society. Departmentalization brought vastly increased health care, which in turn contribu-ted to a decline in child mortality and more rapid population growth.

Population growth and density have received as much attention as any other development in the contemporary period, with the works of Henri Léridon and Yves Charbit on Martinique among the most comprehensive for any Caribbean island. By the 1960s Martinique's population density, already one of the highest in the Caribbean, skyrocketed to more than 750 persons per square mile, a ratio that has been maintained at this already high level only by an equally high emigration from the island to France. For over twenty years more than one-third of all Martinicans have lived in France, where they have formed a cheap labour pool working primarily in the service sector and a source of remittances to those at home. Today there are 350,000 Martinicans living on the island with perhaps an additional 125,000 in France. This widespread emigration to low-paying jobs abroad and the sending of remittances home is a situation which Martinique shares with all the islands of the Lesser Antilles.

Nevertheless, even this exodus from the island has not been sufficient to preserve the peasant way of life that once existed for many African-Americans in highland villages. Michael Horowitz, in a now-classic study conducted in the late 1950s, captured island peasant society just before it began to unravel. Highland villages were then characterized by small subsistence-oriented landholdings, widespread reciprocal ties and obligations, and female-oriented households. Horowitz correctly predicted the disappearance of this life because of population pressure and economic nonviability.

Many island land holdings have, in fact, been subdivided so frequently they have become too small to farm profitably and their owners have left them fallow or for others to work. The exodus to France has been accompanied by a rural-to-urban movement so heavy that the Martinican capital of Fort-de-France now houses more than one-third of all islanders. Many of these migrants have followed a pattern characteristic in most developing countries, one that begins with residence in a spontaneous squatter-settlement and low-paying employment in the informal or service sector. Despite their status as citizens of France, most urban Martinicans are poor and heavily dependent on government programmes. Sociologist Michel LaGuerre has written an insightful study on the mechanisms and institutions that help create and perpetuate urban poverty in Fort-de-France.

Female-centred homes (matrifocality) with children from several fathers (pluripaternity) are common in Martinican society, characteristics it shares with the rest of the Caribbean. Adult women head households in which their elderly mothers and unmarried children reside; they adopt a pattern of sequential conjugality, generally through common-law marriage, with the fathers of their children. The stability of a household, however, rests with the woman. Legal marriage most commonly occurs when land or other real property is involved and men wish to ensure inheritance rights. Miriam Slater and Guy Dubreuil, in studies conducted in the late 1950s and 1960s, focused on these patterns of marriage and family organization that fall outside Western expectations; they have explained such systems in the complex and oppressive social and economic histories of Martinican society. There is, however, a distinct polarity to this society, with one set of rules and social reality for the poor, who are mostly blacks, and quite another for the middle class and well-to-do. The multiple forms of mating and household organization on the island, while well-studied, are complex and not yet thoroughly understood.

Like many Latin American countries, Martinique has been controlled economically, and politically as well, by a few very wealthy landowners, locally called *Békés*, who originally made their fortunes and gained their power through sugar plantations. They are an over-studied group, from their legendary endogamy and economic expansion into milling and finance in the 19th century, to their further diversification into bananas, tourism, and retailing in more recent years. These are all moves that have solidified their power and wealth at a time when other traditional oligarchies have been quite threatened. Indeed, *Békés* have generally been well represented on the French councils that have made policies affecting them, thus guaranteeing their ongoing success in controlling the Martinican economy and prospering from it.

Nonetheless, the perception is widespread among Martinicans and French observers that alone, the island would be economically nonviable. This observation is always made in relationship to metropolitan France, which has enjoyed fifty years of post-war prosperity, and not in comparison with Caribbean neighbours. Employment on the island has changed during the last fifty years from a largely agricultural work force to one predominantly engaged in service sector activities and even off-island jobs. Data which would allow an incisive evaluation of Martinique's economy are not available, but it is widely assumed that for the average Martinican living standards would decline without French social programmes. Whether this assumption is valid has not yet been assessed but what is clear is that many important islanders prefer their French ties, and all they confer, to independence.

Modern Martinique is a curious geographical entity – a fully-fledged member of France but with all the characteristics of a developing country. This is a status that seems unlikely to soon change, for the longer the two remain linked, the more difficult it appears to be for islanders to contemplate independence. Political autonomy seems a more likely outcome, but only when the self-awareness of Martinicans becomes more widely acknowledged and expressed. The fact that Martinique receives the majority of its news, entertainment, and education through French media and publications has surely slowed this process. In addition, a surprising amount of island foodstuffs and other items that could be produced locally are shipped in from France. Articulate spokespersons for Martinican identity and common Caribbean values like Edouard Glissant are not widely read in Martinique and instead find their greatest audience in France. Folk culture in Martinique – zouk music or popular Catholicism, for instance – seems not to have provided a strong political outlet or rallying point as it has on other Caribbean islands. There is a sizeable French bureaucracy in Martinique, which consists of civil servants from the European mainland who administer government health, education, and other social service programmes. They and other mainland French maintain second or vacation homes on the island.The tourist industry, too, is oriented to the French and has been profitably developed by *Béké* capital. All of these whites form the dominant minority in Martinican society which is rigidly stratified by race and class.

The enigma of being French, black, and Caribbean all at the same time has given rise to one of the oldest and richest literary traditions in the region. Several of Martinique's authors are towering international figures. Aimé Césaire, the great surrealist poet and playright, was among the founders of the influential Negritude movement and has been almost synonymous with Martinican politics for the last fifty years. He has long served as mayor of Fort-de-France and as a deputy to the French National Assembly. Frantz Fanon was one of Césaire's students who went on to become a psychiatrist specializing in oppression. He completely disowned his Martinican youth and became more associated with the Algerian struggle for independence from France than with his own Caribbean roots. His essays inspired a generation of Third World revolutionaries and the Black Power movement. By contrast, Edouard Glissant, also a Césaire student, has produced a group of stunning novels which give voice to a black Caribcentric history and worldview. His work occupies for the literary world a place similar to that of Sidney Mintz's among anthropological and sociological studies of the Caribbean in its interpretative significance.

The further enigma of being female in Martinique's Latin environment is giving rise to a recent genre of literary activity, more fully developed in Guadeloupe and elsewhere in the Caribbean, but only in its infancy in Martinique. A sizeable scholarly literature also exists which focuses on women. Because of the matrifocality of Martinican creole society, the extant sociological, demographic, and anthropological literature pays a great deal of attention to women's roles. Women, as elsewhere in the Caribbean, have traditionally controlled dooryard gardens and food markets; childrearing is almost completely a woman's responsibility; and most traditional healers are female. Nevertheless, modern gender theory has yet to be applied to Martinique.

In a society where primary education has long been universal and high quality social services readily available, Martinique's fertility rates resemble those of other developing Caribbean countries and not those of France; employment structure similarly mirrors that of island neighbours; and poverty is widespread. These are among the most apparent and serious legacies of colonialism in Martinique that defy its departmental status, which has now been in effect for more than forty-five years. Arvin Murch caustically refers to France's 'artificial modernization of Martinique' and believes that it and the island's dependence on France has fostered a deep-seated and as yet unexpressed anger among Martinicans.

Martinican literature, unfortunately, has been only patchily translated into English and therefore remains somewhat inaccessible and underappreciated in the English-speaking world. There has been a recent flurry of doctoral dissertations on Césaire's politics and oeuvre, which is testimony to his growing stature in American universities. However, it does seem to be part of a broader interest in the literature of oppression, since all Caribbean writers are enjoying attention in academic circles.

The Bibliography

Written work on Martinique, which is relatively scanty to begin with, is even less accessible to the English reader. Although Caribbean studies have proliferated in the English speaking Caribbean in the last twenty years, Martinique remains under-researched. A handful of Canadian, French, and American scholars have conducted the few systematic studies on the island that exist, but there is a sizeable French-language literature that is of less than first-rate quality. Here is an island with a rich and enigmatic history whose inadequate study invites both the serious scholar and the curious journalist or writer.

French literature on Martinique is surprisingly small, given the island's historical importance and its tropical American location. Thus, although I have not included all existing works in French in this bibliography, the student will find that, other than for literary genres and uninterpreted archival or historical inventories, further bibliographical work will likely uncover few published surprises. This became abundantly clear to me as I examined the numerous bibliographies which have been produced since the advent of computer databases in the late 1980s. The same publications appeared over and over again, regardless of subject peculiarities and the cross-referencing of individual bibliographical categories. With the exception of recent doctoral dissertations, publications in the reference source section here should be considered thorough and comprehensive. One bibliographical work, however, deserves special mention here: the volume edited by Paula Covington on Latin

Introduction

America and the Caribbean includes essays that introduce the user to twenty-one academic disciplines and their current research trends in the region. It provides the best up-to-date perspective on research and literature relating to the Caribbean of which I am aware and it will long remain topical.

I have been inclusive with the available English-language publications on Martinique, many of which are translations from the French, and also with the most important contextual regional literature. Nonetheless a surprising number of the included entries – particularly general studies – are now dated and would benefit from new field observations and updated interpretations. Some examples include Robert Pinchon's overview of Martinican archaeology, written in the early 1950s; Michel Leiris's study of race and society in Martinique, researched in the late 1940s; Eugéne Revert's physical and human geography, drawn from observations in the twenty years prior to 1949; and Michael Horowitz's study of a peasant village in the mid-1950s.

Subject areas truly well represented in the published literature are few: the eruption of Mont Pelée in 1902 and the concurrent destruction of the cosmopolitan financial and cultural centre of St. Pierre on the island's northwest coast; Martinican archaeology and prehistory, in which there are abundant reports on individual sites; literary criticism treating the works of Césaire, Fanon, and Glissant; post-war fertility and emigration trends; and the French policy of assimilation and its dampening effect on an independence movement.

The opportunities for research are even more evident: a definitive history of Martinique has yet to be written. Both the archives of France and the several repositories in Martinique promise rich rewards on both general and specialized topics. Liliane Chauleau has published on these archival resources as well as providing inventories of available documents on Martinique. A cultural geography that focuses on human-environment interactions would be a welcome general work, treating, for example, the changing distributions and influence of Martinique's extremely high population densities. Fort-de-France is a large and growing city, yet I found fewer than half a dozen studies treating any aspect of life there. There is surely a significant flow of remittances to the island by relatives working in France, yet this has received no attention by scholars. We have William Miles's study of Martinican politics and election results in the early 1980s, and the fine monograph on the islanders' overall lack of political vision by Richard Burton, but we could surely learn much from further probing into the political orientation and activities of a wider sample of Martinicans. Publications on similar topics for the English-speaking Caribbean islands have, in the last twenty years, become substantial and would provide valuable points of comparison and contrast.

While there are a number of excellent monographs on aspects of Martinique's history and society listed in this bibliography – particularly the work of Michael Horowitz, Clarissa Kimber, Michel LaGuerre, Claire Lefebvre, and Miriam Slater – what is missing is work from a scholar who has followed Martinican society for a long period of time and who has a personal comparative perspective. Few individuals in the social and behavioural sciences have continued to work on island topics over a long period of time. However, if this is true in the social sciences, it is even more applicable in the biological and environmental areas. Martinique desperately needs detailed studies on its land and marine fauna, forest reserves, coastal landforms and landscapes, vegetational succession, river valleys, and weather patterns.

Martinique still awaits its share of attention from the growing interest in the Caribbean region, especially among English- and German-speaking scholars. Perhaps the language difference has been more effective than one would immediately presume. Even tourism to the island, while on the rise, comes largely from France and a different stream than the North Americans who frequent the English- and Spanish-speaking islands. The tourist movement and its influence has barely been noticed in the literature. This bibliography, with its many obvious omissions, should indicate to both the English- and French-speaking scholar how many basic research areas remain to be investigated on Martinique.

I have looked at all the publications annotated here, primarily using libraries in and around Boston, Massachusetts. I have depended particularly on the fine collections of the Boston Public Library and the libraries of Harvard University; but I have also used the libraries at Bunker Hill Community College, Salem State College, Tufts University, and the University of Connecticut. I am grateful for the interlibrary loan services and courteous help they provided me. With access to a major university collection and an interlibrary loan service, I believe that the diligent scholar should be able to obtain copies of any of the items listed here. I wish to thank Riva Berleant-Schiller for making available many articles and books from her personal collection. Thank you also to Arnold Berleant, Riva Berleant-Schiller, Steve Crowson, and Jon Papps for the many ways they supported me in this project.

Janet Crane
Salem, Massachusetts, USA
August 1994

The Department and Its People

1 **Caribbean isles.**
    Peter Wood. New York: Time, 1975. 184 p.
This book is a coffee-table natural history, in which the author anecdotally describes island life, wildlife, reef life, and the environment. There is a superb black-and-white photo essay on the Mont Pelée eruption of 1902 on Martinique.

2 **The Caribbean region.**
    Sidney Mintz. In: *Slavery, colonialism, and racism.* Edited by Sidney W. Mintz. New York: W. W. Norton & Company, 1974,
    p. 45-71.
Mintz describes the Caribbean as a 'patchwork quilt of societies, each one a patchwork itself, the whole a foreign invention'. In this chapter he discusses the parallel demographic, racial, economic, and political histories of the various islands that provide a regional framework. At the same time he identifies the considerable cultural and social diversity from island to island within this larger region. Finally, he points to several recent developments which give greater definition to the region: the emerging self-characterization of the Caribbean by native-born writers and scholars; new directions and topics in Afro-Caribbeanist research; and the massive ongoing migration of Caribbean peoples to Europe and North America. The entire chapter is a pertinent introduction to Martinique's regional milieu.

3 **Love in the Caribbean.**
    Alec Waugh. New York: Paragon House, 1991, 310p.
This reprinted volume contains material first published in 1929 and 1930 and is aimed at the armchair traveller. Waugh, best known as a novelist, spent many years in the Caribbean and had a particular fondness for Martinique. One chapter in this book is specifically on Martinique, but there are references to the island throughout. Waugh is highly readable and an observant writer.

4 **Martinique.**
   Hans W. Hannau.   Garden City, New Jersey: Doubleday & Company,
   1967. 60 p.

Generalized basic geographical and historical information on the island is provided in this small format picture book. It is a romanticized account of Martinique's past and present under the veneer of enlightened French policy and tropical island charm.

5 **Martinique, a tropical bit of France.**
   Gwen Drayton Allmon.   *National Geographic Magazine*, vol. 115,
   no. 2 (Feb. 1959), p. 255-83.

This breezy, journalistic account of a short stay on the island provides the reader with an overview of touristic Martinique. Photographs record cane and sugar operations in 1959.

6 **La Martinique, carrefour du Monde caraïbe.** (Martinique, crossroads of the Caribbean.)
   Auguste Joyau.   Fort-de-France, Martinique: Editions des Horizons
   Caraïbes, 1967. 172 p.

A surprising amount of information on Martinique is brought together in this volume in a form accessible to the nonspecialist who reads descriptive French. After an introductory history, the author briefly treats each of Martinique's thirty-four communes. There is also a lengthy discussion of Martinican literature and authors followed by sections on island art and folklore.

7 **Martinique: liberté, egalité, and uncertainty in the Caribbean.**
   Kenneth MacLeish.   *National Geographic Magazine*, vol. 147,
   no. 2 (Jan. 1975), p. 124-48.

In this article the author offers a quite general descriptive survey of Martinique's past, its people and their social status, the island economy, and its political status.

8 **The West Indies.**
   Harman Carter and the editors of *Life*.   New York: Time Incorporated,
   1966. 160p.

This volume is part of the Life World Library Series and is aimed at a wide general readership. It is a competently-written general survey of the Caribbean region for the nonspecialist in which the author attempts to generalize about the shared characteristics of many Caribbean islands. At the same time he brings out certain historical, political, and economic issues peculiar to individual islands. Martinique is well represented in both text and photographs.

Geography

Regional and general

9 **The Caribbean in the wider world, 1492-1992.**
    Bonham C. Richardson.   Cambridge, England; New York; Port Chester;
    Melbourne; Sydney: Cambridge University Press, 1992. 235p. bibliog.
This regional geography is a textbook survey that explores how the Caribbean's
present is intimately linked to its past, and is best understood in terms of relationships
with Europe and the United States. Sections are devoted to colonizations, economic
enterprises and resulting dependencies, human migrations, United States political
interventions and influences, and political independence and nationship. The book
provides a comprehensive overview and an excellent framework in which to place any
Martinican study. There are many references to Martinican examples of more widespread regional characteristics.

10 **The Caribbean islands.**
    Helmut Blume.   London: Longman, 1974. 464p. maps. bibliog.
This represents a basic regional geography of the Caribbean islands. Part one includes
the physical environment, native American populations, the colonial period, demography, agricultural systems, and the regional economy. Chapters of Part two are
devoted to individual islands and island groups, providing information on physical,
historical, agricultural, and population data. The book is a good general source
on rural land use in the Caribbean. The section on Martinique includes a cross-section
on Mont Pelée's rainfall and vegetative environments.

11 **The Lesser Antilles.**
    W. M. Davis.   New York: The American Geographical Society of New
    York, 1926. 207p.
A physiographic description and analysis of all the islands of the Lesser Antilles,
including Martinique, is provided in this small volume. Morris adheres to a systematic sequence of island development in which each island fits a particular stage. Island

landform features are the keys to determining the stage in the sequence to which it belongs. The author describes the mountains, valleys, sea-cliffs, and coral reefs of Martinique as belonging to a 'more complicated sequence of first-cycle islands'. More recent research in plate tectonics, vulcanology, and physical geomorphology has provided explanatory theories that supersede much of this work but Davis's ideas on sea-level changes and island subsidence are still useful in interpreting landforms and reefs. The line drawings of coastlines are a valuable part of the volume.

12 **La Martinique: étude géographique et humaine.** (Martinique: geographical and human study.)
Eugéne Revert. Paris: Nouvelles éditions latines, 1949. 559p. bibliog.

This volume was the first attempt at a truly systematic and comprehensive regional geography of Martinique. The author was stationed on Martinique in various governmental posts for almost twenty years from the 1920s to the 1940s. The first part of the book is devoted to physical geography and includes sections on the 1929-32 eruption of Mont Pelée, volcanic terrains, geomorphology, climate, surface and subterranean water, and vegetation. The section on human geography contains chapters on the peopling and settlement of the island, agriculture, industry, commerce and the economy. The final chapter on Martinican life deals with folklore, festivals, social customs, and race questions. This account is based more on observation and description than data collection and systematic analysis, but it is a competent overview of the island in the pre-Second World War period.

13 **Middle America. Its lands and peoples.**
Robert C. West, John P. Augelli. Englewood Cliffs, New Jersey: Prentice-Hall, 1989. 3rd ed. 494p.

The West Indies and Martinique form part of Middle America, for which this text is the standard geography. The authors' distinctive interpretation is an historical-geographical one which identifies cultural and environmental patterns that have evolved and changed through time. One chapter each is devoted to the geographical aspects of West Indian history, economy, and population and geopolitics. Although there are common threads in West Indian history and geography, each island has a certain individuality and uniqueness. This constitutes an excellent general work for the non-specialist and contains a brief section solely on the French West Indies.

14 **Réunion et la Martinique.** (Réunion and Martinique.)
Hildebert Isnard. *Les Cahiers d'Outre-Mer*, vol. 9, no. 33 (1956), p. 58-69.

The author begins this article by pointing out the many similarities that Martinique and Réunion share: both are tropical volcanic islands, have an introduced lowland vegetation, are planted to sugarcane monoculture, have a multiracial creole population without indigenes, and are now thoroughly 'French' as overseas departments. Nevertheless, the differences are also numerous and significant and stem from island size, altitude, habitat differentiation, rainfall, population density, and a host of other physical and cultural factors. This process of comparing and contrasting proves to be a good device to help one understand patterns and processes in shaping both similarity and uniqueness on inhabited oceanic islands.

15 The West Indies: patterns of development, culture and environmental change since 1492.
David Watts. Cambridge, England: Cambridge University Press, 1987. 609p. maps. bibliog.

This volume is a definitive study of the historical geography of the West Indies and focuses on the evolution and spread of the sugar plantation in the region. Although one chapter treats the aboriginal population and land use, the majority of the book deals with the sweeping demographic and environmental changes that followed the European invasion in 1492. The entire study is pertinent to Martinique's history and landscape and contains numerous references to the island which deal particularly with the sizes of landholdings and population growth and characteristics.

Soil

16 Soil associations on volcanic material in tropical America with special reference to Martinique and Guadeloupe.
F. Colmet-Daage, J. Gautheyron. *Tropical Agriculture*, vol. 51, no. 2 (April 1974), p. 121-28.

Soil groups derived from volcanic ash of different elevations, exposures, and ages on Martinique are described in this article. The authors find that the properties of soils and mineralogical composition of clays are closely linked in these moderately-evolved island soil associations. Moisture content and the presence of gibbsite serve as a synthesis of many soil properties and demonstrate their age as well. The results obtained on Martinique are compared to similar studies on Guadeloupe and on volcanic and non-volcanic soils elsewhere in tropical America.

Climate and weather

17 Cindy rocks Martinique.
The Washington Post, 16 August 1993. p. A4.

This brief article reports on the tropical storm 'Cindy', which hit Martinique on 15 August 1993, bringing high winds and heavy rains to the island. At least one death resulted.

18 La tempête tropicale "Dorothy" à la Martinique (20-21 août 1970).
(Tropical storm "Dorothy" in Martinique [20-21 August 1970].)
Jean-Michel Sirivine. *Les Cahiers d'Outre-Mer*, vol. 25, no. 99 (1972), p. 338-46.

Diagrams and satellite imagery supplement this brief text, which reviews the development of the tropical storm 'Dorothy' that wreaked havoc on Martinique, and the capital city of Fort-de-France in particular. The strong vertical development of the storm and the amphitheatre-like nature of the terrain on which the city and its suburbs are constructed, contributed to the unusual local distribution of the extremely heavy rainfall that accompanied the storm.

Atlases and maps

19 **Atlas of Central America and the Caribbean.**
   The Diagram Group. New York: MacMillan Publishing Company, 1985. 144p.

This is a useful reference work for the nonspecialist. Part one is a regional profile that includes maps and data on ocean patterns, climate, biota, prehistory, and colonial culture and economy. Parts two and three present current regional population, land use, political and financial maps and data for Central America and the Caribbean in addition to more detailed information for their constituent entities. Four pages are devoted to the French Antilles, with thumbnail historical and economic reviews.

20 **Atlas historique du patrimoine sucrier de la Martinique.** (Historical atlas of Martinique's sugar legacy.)
   Mireille Mousnier, Brigitte Caille. Paris: L'Harmattan, 1990. 104p. maps.

Mousnier and Caille examine resources that permit a reconstruction of Martinique's sugar landscape and industry from the 17th century to the present. The first chapter describes old maps of Martinique from the richest collections in Martinique and France. Sixteen plates of portions of these maps are reproduced, giving an idea of the information they contain. Chapter two treats cartographic representations as they became more scientific through time; increased detail on maps includes buildings and toponyms related to the sugar industry. The third chapter details the six maps compiled by the authors from cartographic sources and which accompany the book. These include: sugar buildings in the 17th and 18th centuries; distilleries at the end of the 19th century; transportation networks and sugar about 1900; and sugar mills and distilleries from 1940-85. The book presents spatially the growth, diversification, and decline of the sugar industry over the last 300 years. It also includes a table listing all plantation names and sites for each of Martinique's thirty-four communes for the years 1670, 1770, 1820, 1882, and 1955.

Geology of Martinique.
See item no. 37.

Travellers' Accounts

21 **Black Martinique - Red Guiana.**
    Nicol Smith.   Indianapolis, New York: Bobbs-Merrill Company, 1942.
    312p.
This travel book emphasizes the 'exoticism' of the tropics and employs unusual personal stories to present a romantic view of Martinique and French Guiana. The author travelled there in 1941, when these then-French colonies were virtually off-limits to Americans. It is this type of book, however, that, by ignoring social and economic conditions, contributes to socially unaware tourism and adventure travel.

22 **Cosimo Brunetti: three relations of the West Indies in 1659-60.**
    Susan Heller Anderson.   *Transactions of the American Philosophical Society*, new series, vol. 59, part 6 (1969). p. 3-49.
Three manuscripts written by the Sienese priest and traveller, Cosimo Brunetti, about his voyage to the West Indies – but in particular to Martinique – are reproduced here. Brunetti had been sent by Port-Royal, a Jansenist movement under persecution by French Jesuits, to inspect Martinique with a view to a possible relocation of its convent there. The manuscripts are valuable for the comments on Martinique's commercial situation, political environment, and colonist life. They reveal a complicated political situation on the island, insights into the costs of transportation and slave trade, as well as an undisguised disdain for the unsophisticated native Caribs living on the island.

23 **Au pays du sucre.** (In the land of sugar.)
    Marcel Dumoret.   Paris: H.-E. Martin, 1902. 224p.
This travel account was written by a Martinican entertaining a French childhood friend for some three months in 1899. Much of the book is written in the form of a dialogue as the two travel to cane plantations, beaches, mangroves, and many other still standard tourist attractions on the island.

24 **The islands and the sea. Five centuries of nature writing from the Caribbean.**
Edited by John A. Murray. New York; Oxford: Oxford University Press, 1991. 329p.

Two excerpts specific to Martinique are included in this anthology. 'La Pelée', from Lafcadio Hearn's *Two Years in the French West Indies*, describes the volcano and an ascent to its top in 1887. Hearn's prose, while effusive to the modern reader, is at once an informative, accurate, and sensitive description of the altitudinal variation in the physical environment. Two of Hearn's sketches are included. 'The Tragedy of Pelée', from the book of the same name by George Kennan, records the testimony of two eye-witnesses taken down shortly after the volcano's great eruption of 1902. Kennan, a journalist who went with the United States expedition sent to the island immediately after the disaster, also vividly describes the ruins of the totally destroyed city of St. Pierre. Both of the books from which these excerpts are drawn are annotated elsewhere in this bibliography.

25 **John Candler's visit to Martinique, Dominica, and Guadeloupe.**
John Candler. *Caribbean Studies*, vol. 5, no. 2 (1965), p. 56-63.

John Candler and his wife, who were Protestant missionaries, spent eight days on Martinique in February of 1850. This was just a little more than a year after the emancipation of slaves on the island. Their observations, made in hospitals, prisons, and on several plantations in and near St. Pierre, are particularly concerned with the overall status of freed slaves and the economic effects of emancipation on planters.

26 **Martinique, Caribbean question mark.**
Edward T. Folliard. *National Geographic Magazine*, vol. 79, no. 1 (1941), p. 47-55.

The author muses on the status of Martinique, caught in limbo with the fall of France in 1940. He visited the island when two French warships were anchored at Fort-de-France to protect the colony and the island's export economy had come to a halt as a result of the British blockade to France. This account consists mostly of photographs.

27 **The Middle Passage.**
V. S. Naipaul. London: André Deutsch, 1962. 232p.

This travel account by the well-known Trinidadian writer records his experiences and impressions during a 1961 journey among five Caribbean societies, one of which is Martinique. In the chapter on the island Naipaul describes Martinique's thoroughly French ambience and the sentiment among islanders that France's colonial policy of assimilation had been successfully achieved there. Naipaul encounters a persistent and heightened degree of racial consciousness – a minute and tiresome class subdivision based on skin colour – he had not experienced elsewhere in the region. He meets a poor couple with Tamil East Indian origins and compares their degraded situation with that of the more culturally vibrant Indian populations of Trinidad and Guyana.

28 **The traveller's tree.**
Patrick Leigh Fermor. London: John Murray, 1950. 403p.

A post-Second World War travel account, this is about six months spent in the Caribbean. The book is well-written in a breezy journalistic, but keenly observant manner. Two chapters are devoted to Martinique and contain Fermor's impressions of the people, folk dances, food and drink, French influence, and the Empress Josephine's childhood home.

29 Two years in the French West Indies.

Lafcadio Hearn. New York: Harper & Brothers, 1890, 431p.

This book is one of the classic 19th-century travel accounts of Martinique. Hearn spent two years on the island between 1887 and 1889. Many of the volume's chapters were originally written as sketches for *Harper's Magazine*. They cover a range of topics on Martinique's landscape; the local people; and creole life, language, and livelihoods. This is still a most readable and informative work.

30 The West Indies.

C. Washington Eves. London: Sampson Low, Marston, Seale, & Rivington, 1889. 322p. maps. illus.

The section on Martinique (p. 235-39) includes a sketch of Martinique's history from the British imperial point of view. The island is described as it was in 1887, with an emphasis on sugar production, imports and exports, immigration, and the labour force. One valuable feature of this brief account is its description of St. Pierre, written before the city was destroyed by the eruption of Mont Pelée in 1902.

31 The West Indies in 1837.

Joseph Sturge, Thomas Harvey. London: Hamilton, Adams & Co., 1838. 380p. appendices, 95p.

The travellers who wrote this volume intended it to present the conditions of apprenticeship, an intermediate step to the full emancipation of slaves, in the British colonies of the Caribbean where it had taken effect in 1833. In transit, they spent several days on Martinique, where emancipation was actively talked about but not yet realized. They report (p. 108-15) on the atmosphere in St. Pierre and Fort Royal (now Fort-de-France), where there was much speculation about when emancipation would occur and its potential effects. The authors comment on the military force which was established in Martinique to prevent the escape of slaves to nearby British islands, to which some 3,000 slaves had already fled. Sturge and Harvey favourably compare the demeanour of Martinican slaves to slave demeanour in the British colonies. Appendix C includes two petitions by coloured proprietors of slaves on Martinique for immediate emancipation.

Geology

Regional and general

32 **Andesites of the Lesser Antilles.**
    W. G. Rea. *Proceedings of the Geological Society of London*,
    no. 1,662 (24 September 1969), p. 39-46.

Both basalt and andesites are connected with vulcanism in the Lesser Antilles, but recent eruptions of Mont Pelée on Martinique have been composed almost entirely of andesite and dacite. This brief report considers the chemical composition, petrogenesis, and the magmatic evolution of Lesser Antillean volcanic materials. The author concludes that basalts and andesites in the islands are closely related, being similar in origin and chemical composition, and are not quite as different as previously maintained. This is a technical article for the geologist or landform specialist.

33 **Caribbean volcanoes: a field guide – Martinique, Dominica, and St. Vincent.**
    Haraldur Sigurdsson, Steven Carey.   Toronto, Canada: Geological Association of Canada, 1991. 101p.

This volume is a comprehensive geological field guide to Martinique, Dominica, and St. Vincent for the knowledgeable geoscientist or enthusiast seeking a scholarly summary of the most recent literature or desiring to visit sites on the islands. The first chapter summarizes recent research in geology and vulcanology of the Lesser Antillean arc and its relationship to surrounding geological features. The second chapter is devoted to Martinique, focusing on the formation of Mont Pelée and the type of eruptions characteristic of this volcano.

34   **An earthquake catalogue for the eastern Caribbean 1530-1960.**
     G. R. Robson.   *Bulletin of the Seismological Society of America,*
     vol. 54, no. 2 (1964), p. 785-832.

This briefly annotated catalogue lists all the eastern Caribbean earthquakes which
were felt or caused damage and were reported in the seismological literature or in
West Indian newspapers. The catalogue is primarily concerned with earthquake
histories of the Lesser Antillean islands, and includes a complete accounting for
Martinique.

35   **The formation of the Lesser Antilles.**
     W. M. Davis.   *Proceedings of the National Academy of Sciences,*
     vol. 10, no. 6 (June 15, 1924), p. 205-11.

A short paper, this begins with a descriptive overview of the submarine banks, volcanic islands, coral reefs, calcareous islands, and uplifted atolls of the Lesser Antilles.
Davis, a pioneer in processual geomorphology and landform development, then outlines a scheme of island development and genetic classification, placing Martinique as
a larger composite island. Martinique's recent cones and mudflows have covered
earlier formed banks and still earlier volcanic forms.

36   **Geological evolution of the Caribbean region: a plate-tectonic
     perspective.**
     James L. Pindell, Stephen F. Barrett.   In: *The Caribbean region.*
     Edited by Gabriel Dengo, J. E. Case.   Boulder, Colorado: Geological
     Society of America, 1990. Vol. H (*The Geology of North America*),
     p. 405-32.

This chapter provides a regional overview of contemporary geological and geophysical knowledge of the Caribbean, into which Martinique can be placed. The Caribbean
tectonic plate, on which Martinique sits, is currently moving east, relative to North
and South America, at between one and three inches a year. As it overrides the westward-moving Atlantic plate, there is vulcanism and island formation on its eastern
margins and a subduction of the Atlantic lithosphere (with oceanic troughs and trenches) farther east. The article is technical for anyone not familiar with recent (post-1969)
plate tectonic hypotheses and data, but it is an invaluable reference and crucial to
understanding regional geological processes and patterns.

37   **Géologie de la Martinique.** (Geology of Martinique.)
     Henri Grunevald.   Paris: Imprimerie National, 1964. 144p. maps.

Originally presented as a doctoral dissertation, this monograph is a useful composite
geological treatment of Martinique and its regional context as understood in 1964.
Grunevald considers the history of geological studies on the island, active and inactive
volcanoes, petrography of widespread rock types, sedimentary terrain containing fos-
sils, and sedimentary outcrops. A pullout, coloured schematic geological map of
Martinique with a 1:100,000 scale accompanies the text. This study just predates the
publication of many studies utilizing new methodologies and geophysical information
that explain Martinique in a plate-tectonic and seafloor-spreading context; it is therefore useful but needs to be supplemented by more recent geological studies.

38 **Geology of the Lesser Antilles.**
R. C. Maury, G. K. Westbrook, et al. In: *The Caribbean Region.*
Edited by Gabriel Dengo, J. E. Case. Boulder, Colorado: The
Geological Society of America, 1990. Vol. H (*The Geology of North
America*), p. 141-66.

The Lesser Antilles form one of two active island arcs of the Atlantic Ocean. This
chapter summarizes all available recent knowledge on the geology and geophysics of
the chain. It covers the crustal structure, pre-Eocene basement, the Limestone
Caribees, the southern volcanic Caribees (of which Martinique is one), and the northern volcanic Caribees. The research synthesized here includes bathymetric
measurements, gravity anomaly patterns, seismic refraction data that show plate con-
vergence, ages of sequential volcanism, and the widespread faulting on and around
Martinique. Because of Martinique's position in the arc it is not only the largest island
with the most complex geological patterns, it is also the site at which the inner (volcanic) arc and the outer (limestone) arc diverge to the north. This is a
state-of-knowledge report, which incorporates the deep-sea drilling data and plate tectonics theories that have shaped the modern era of Caribbean geology.

39 **Geophysical investigations in the Eastern Caribbean.**
C. B. Officer, et al. *Bulletin of the Geological Society of America*, vol.
68 (March 1957), p. 359-78.

This article is among the earliest to incorporate seafloor geophysical measurements in
the Eastern Caribbean. By means of seismic refraction data the authors show that the
Caribbean Basin, which includes the Lesser Antilles, has a significantly different crustal structure to the Atlantic Basin. The authors consider the origin of the deep sea
trenches east of the Antilles, the island arc, and the altered Caribbean Basin to be
related phenomena. In the Eastern Caribbean, compression is occurring and the lighter
Caribbean crust is overriding the heavier Atlantic material, with associated vulcanism,
earthquakes, and crustal fracturing. This concise study of the Eastern Caribbean,
where two tectonic plates are converging, provides the context for understanding
Martinique's geology and placement in the region.

40 **Gravity anomalies and island arc structure with particular
reference to the West Indies.**
Harry Hammond Hess. *Proceedings of the American Philosophical
Society*, vol. 79, no. 1 (1938), p. 71-96.

The author applies the discovery of the relationship between huge gravity anomalies
and the building of island arcs to the Caribbean Basin. A strip of strong negative
anomalies runs just east of the Lesser Antilles. In this regional geophysical and geological study, the author concludes that the Lesser Antilles, including Martinique, are
on an anticline and represent the structural connection between the Venezuelan east-
west ranges and the Greater Antilles.

41 **Historical geology of the Antillean-Caribbean region.**
Charles Schuchert. New York: Wiley & Sons; London: Chapman &
Hall. 1935. 811p. bibliog.

This volume is the first attempt to provide a regional historical geology for the lands
bordering the Caribbean and the Gulf of Mexico. The initial sections deal with

regional geological features, mountain building, paleogeography, structural basins, and biogeography. In the detailed sections on smaller subregions that comprise the bulk of the book, Martinique is described as an oceanic island, one of the younger volcanic Caribees. This now-dated volume – dated because it precedes the seafloor studies and plate tectonic work of the 1970s – is useful nonetheless, because it represents a thorough history of geological research and theory affecting Martinique prior to 1935. Although Schuchert did not believe the Caribees (Lesser Antilles) had ever been a land bridge between the Antilles and South America, there was not yet conclusive geophysical evidence to thoroughly put those theories to rest.

42 **The Lesser Antilles and Aves Ridge.**
John Frederick Tomblin. In: *The Gulf of Mexico and the Caribbean*, vol. 3 of *The ocean basins and margins*. Edited by Alan E. M. Nairn, Francis G. Stehli. New York; London: Plenum Press. 1975.
p. 444-500.

Research on the volcanic history, petrography, and geophysics of the Lesser Antilles, of which Martinique is a part, is synthesized in this chapter. All data indicate crustal subduction occurring now along the island arc. This is a useful chapter because it looks at complexity within the Lesser Antilles and gives information to account for differing seismicity, vulcanism, and rock types in three distinct zones: the section from Montserrat north; the central segment of which Martinique is the southernmost island; and the tier from St. Lucia south.

43 **Petrology of the volcanic rocks of Martinique, West Indies.**
D. Westercamp. *Bulletin Volcanologique*, vol. 39, no. 2 (1975).
p. 175-200.

This paper considers the petrography and petrochemistry of the two categories of lava occurring on Martinique. The first series is older, substratum material, primarily a high alumina basalt. This is the most important lava series from a quantitative standpoint, but has received little attention because it doesn't include the recent products of Mont Pelée. The second series, the calc-alkaline (slightly potassic) series composed of andesites and dacites, is found only among recent volcanics, best known from Mont Pelée's 1902 and 1929 eruptions. The author discusses the time-sequence of the different lavas.

44 **Physiography of the Gulf of Mexico and Caribbean Sea.**
Elazar Uchupi. In: *The Gulf of Mexico and the Caribbean*, vol. 3 of *The ocean basins and margins*. Edited by Alan E. M. Nairn, Francis G. Stehli. New York; London: Plenum Press. 1975. p. 1-64.

The author describes the physiography, origin, and evolution of the Caribbean as an inland sea, using data from deep sea drilling, bathymetric charts, and seismic reflection work of the 1960s and 1970s. The Lesser Antilles form the boundary where the rigid eastward-moving Caribbean plate is being underthrust by the west-moving North American plate and are part of a region characterized by the most diverse topography in the Atlantic Basin.

45 **Volcanoes.**
Peter Francis. Harmondsworth, England: Penguin Books, 1976. 368p.
This highly readable volume presents the latest geophysical research on volcanoes and discusses the natural resources and hazards associated with areas of active vulcanism. The 1902 eruption of Mont Pelée is one of three thoroughly described classic eruptions. The discussion of *nuées ardentes*, or glowing clouds, first described and recognized in connection with Mont Pelée, and the inclusion of numerous photos and diagrams of Martinique's volcanic landscape, make this a useful volume for the nonspecialist.

Mont Pelée

46 **Bibliography of literature of the West Indian eruptions published in the United States.**
Edmund Otis Hovey. *Bulletin of the Geological Society of America*, vol. 15 (Dec. 1904), p. 562-66.
Both Mont Pelée on Martinique and La Soufrière on St. Vincent experienced catastrophic eruptions in May of 1902. This bibliography lists the many English-language US publications that followed the eruptions, covering the period May 1902 through October 1904. The accounts are by both journalists and geologists.

47 **A comparison of the recent eruptions of Mt. Pelée, Martinique, and Soufrière, St. Vincent.**
M. J. Roobol, A. L. Smith. *Bulletin Volcanologique*, vol. 39, no. 2 (1976), p. 214-40.
The authors describe the 1902 eruptions of the two volcanoes, the 1929-32 eruptions of Mont Pelée, and the eruption of Soufrière in 1971-72. They also describe and analyse the resulting deposits, domes, mudflows, petrography, and varied chemistry of the deposits. The striking differences in the styles of eruptions and materials extruded are explained in the context of plate tectonics and ongoing plate movements. The authors demonstrate that Pelée tapped a deep level magma chamber, which resulted in its extreme heat and violence, whereas the Soufrière eruptions extruded material from chambers of varying, but shallower depths. Charts with detailed chronological summaries of both of Pelée's eruptions are included.

48 **The day the world ended.**
Gordon Thomas, Max Morgan Witts. New York: Stein & Day, 1969, 308p.
This volume recounts the seven days leading to and including the devastating eruption of Mont Pelée on 8 May 1902, in which the city of St. Pierre was destroyed. It is written in a dramatic style and is based on eyewitness interviews and contemporary records. The authors conclude that the deaths of nearly 30,000 people could have been avoided. The text gives accounts of the activities of those public officials who, in the authors' view, in some fashion 'had a hand' in the tragedy.

49 **Mont Pelée.**

André Midas. *Caribbean Commission Monthly Information Bulletin*, vol. 8, no. 1 (1954), p. 7-8, 12.

In this short, lively account Mont Pelée and the surrounding countryside, including the city of St. Pierre, are described, before the 1902 eruption and during the 1950s. The article is worthy of note for its incorporation of impressions on the Mont Pelée region by a variety of travel writers and academic observers.

50 **Mt. Pelée and the island population of Martinique.**

M. J. Roobol, Roget H. Petitjean, A. L. Smith. *Proceedings of the Sixth International Congress for the Study of pre-Columbian Cultures of the Lesser Antilles.* Gainesville, Florida: Florida State Museum, 1976, p. 46-53.

This article, written by two geologists and an archaeologist, attempts to relate Mont Pelée's eruptions to prehistoric populations on Martinique. The authors describe the several types of eruptions associated with Pelée: pumice flows and *nuées ardentes* are violent but rarely affect the entire area around the volcano; airflow pyroclastic eruptions are cooler, less destructive, and produce well-sorted materials that are generally associated with the best farmland near the volcano. The remainder of the article reports on stratigraphic sections containing prehistoric artifacts, with the objective of further determining the frequency, type, and territorial extent of various eruptions. The authors speculate on how past eruptions may have influenced Amerindian settlement and migration on Martinique.

51 **Mont Pelée and the tragedy of Martinique.**

Angelo Heilprin. Philadelphia; London: J. B. Lippincott Company, 1903. 335p.

The author, president of the Geographical Society of Philadelphia, arrived on Martinique on 25 May, 1902, shortly after the eruption of May 8th, and visited again three months later. This book is both an account of his impressions of the 1902 eruptions and an attempt to put them in historical and geological perspective. In one chapter he compares the 1902 destruction of St. Pierre on Martinique with that of Pompeii and Vesuvius. Later, he compares Pelée with other contemporary eruptions and describes phenomena such as the ash cloud, magnetic disturbances, and superheated steam that distinguish Pelée's activity.

52 **Mt. Pelée, Martinique.**

Alan L. Smith, M. John Roobol. Boulder, Colorado: Geological Society of America, 1990. 105p. bibliog.

The Lesser Antillean volcanic arc, of which Martinique is at the mid-point, is the surface manifestation of a subduction zone: along this zone the North American tectonic plate is under-thrusting the Caribbean plate and volcanic activity is common. Eruptions of Mont Pelée, Martinique's only active volcano, are comprised of huge ash clouds, pyroclastic flows, and dome building. This volume examines types of deposits, petrography, mineralogy, and Pelée's volcanic history, with reconstructions of the past 14,000 years from radiocarbon deposits. It includes a simplified and updated geological map that illustrates the basic stratigraphy of Martinique.

53 **Mount Pelée, Martinique: a pattern of alternating eruptive styles.**
M. J. Roobol, A. L. Smith. *Geology*, vol. 4, no. 9 (Sept. 1976),
p. 521-24.

This brief article classifies the volcaniclastic deposits associated with Mont Pelée on
Martinique, of which some ten distinctive types are represented. This classification is
then used in the construction of stratigraphic sections measured on the volcano. The
authors conclude that Mont Pelée's stratigraphy shows that the volcano has been built
by alternating episodes of *nuée ardente* deposits and pumiceous deposits.

54 **Pelé and the evolution of the windward archipelago.**
Robert T. Hill. *Bulletin of the Geological Society of America*, vol. 16
(1905), p. 243-88.

The author of this paper, a geologist, represented the National Geographic Society in
covering Mont Pelée's 1902 eruption. This report, issued three years later, represents a
composite of all accounts and knowledge gained from studies of both Pelée and
Soufrière on St. Vincent, which erupted almost simultaneously. Hill considers the contemporary geological literature, prevailing theories of vulcanism, and variation in
volcanic activity in the Lesser Antilles.

55 **The tragedy of Pelée.**
George Kennan. New York: The Outlook Company, 1902. Reprinted,
Negro Universities Press, 1969. 257p.

This little volume is now a classic among travellers' accounts of Martinique. Kennan,
a journalist for *The Outlook*, arrived on the island less than two weeks after the tragic
eruption of Mont Pelée on 8 May 1902. This account describes the mud, ash, and rock
flows as well as the effects of the high heat, gas, and dust connected with the eruption.
Kennan's description of the completely destroyed city of St. Pierre, interviews with
many eyewitnesses and the lone survivor of that disaster, and his own adventure during the later 26 May eruption, make for lively reading, even ninety years later.

Flora and Fauna

56 **Birds of the West Indies.**
James Bond. Boston: Houghton Mifflin, 1986. 5th American ed. 256p. maps.

This is the standard field guide to birds of the West Indies. Every known species, more than 400 in total, is described and information on local names, plumage, nesting, habitat, breeding, songs, and range is also provided. Most of the resident species are depicted by either black-and-white line drawings or coloured plates. This book is useful for the specialist and nonspecialist alike.

57 **Caribbean reef fishes.**
John E. Randall. Neptune City, New Jersey: T. F. H. Publications, 1983. 350p.

Formal descriptions and illustrations are provided in this field guide of the 300 species most likely to be encountered in Caribbean waters, with less comprehensive treatment of an additional 100 species. The book is designed for scuba divers and snorkellers, but will be useful to fishermen and biologists as well.

58 **Caribbean reef invertebrates and plants.**
Patrick L. Colin. Neptune City, New Jersey: T. F. H. Publications, 1978. 512p. bibliog.

This field guide is designed to facilitate the identification of common reef invertebrates and plants found in Caribbean waters; it will be useful to the professional biologist and to recreational divers and snorkellers. It is well illustrated with photographs of species in their natural habitat. The text gives ecological and distributional information as well as references to the scholarly literature.

59   A field guide to the butterflies of the West Indies.

Norman D. Riley.   London: Collins Publications, 1975. 224p.

All the butterflies of the Caribbean islands, including Martinique, are included in this illustrated field guide. Each of the 293 species is described and illustrated, and information on distribution, early stages, subspecies, distinctive markings, and behaviour is included. This is the most complete identification guide available, and will be useful for the specialist and nonspecialist; it includes a checklist and distribution table for the Windward Islands (which include Martinique).

60   A field guide to coral reefs of the Caribbean and Florida.

Eugene H. Kaplan.   Boston: Houghton Mifflin Company, 1982. 289p.

(The Peterson Field Guide Series.)

This compact field guide is arranged by coral reef communities and reef zones, and also by groups of similar inhabiting species. It covers the majority of forms likely to be encountered near most Caribbean coral reefs. The book is designed to aid the nonspecialist in field identifications and contains many keys to the separation of confusing look-alikes. There is also information on behaviour, natural history, and ecology. Some 35 plates, 124 figures, a glossary, and an index make this an easy-to-use yet comprehensive guide for the more than 500 species covered.

61   Flora of the Lesser Antilles. Leeward and Windward Islands.

Richard A. Howard.   Jamaica Plain, Massachusetts: Arnold Arboretum, Harvard University, 1974-89. 6 vols. bibliog.

An ambitious and magnificent work, this fulfils the need for a single, all-encompassing floristic survey of all the Lesser Antilles. It brings together information not only from all previously published floras of the various political and linguistic island groups, but adds much new information from collections and classification conducted by the author and his colleagues. Each entry lists the herbarium in which the type specimen is located and the publication where the species was first described. The distribution for each species in the Lesser Antilles is indicated by listing island names, which include Martinique, on which specimens have been collected. Each genus is represented by a drawing of at least one member species. This is the definitive work for the specialist, although the well-informed nonspecialist wishing to go beyond all but the most common trees and flowers will also find this series invaluable. Each of the six volumes has an index to the scientific names covered in the volume. The set includes: Volume 1, *Orchidaceae* (orchids); Volume 2, *Pteridophyta* (ferns); Volume 3, *Monocotyledoneae* (monocots); and Volumes 4-6, *Dicotyledoneae* (dicots).

62   The flora of Martinique.

Henri Stehlé.   *Journal of the New York Botanical Garden*, vol. 42, no. 502 (1941), p. 235-44.

This article begins with a short descriptive survey of Martinique's three natural vegetation zones. There follows a discussion of introduced cultivated plants and their areas of origin. Stehlé provides a general introductory overview for the nonspecialist.

63 **Flore illustrée des phanérogames de Guadeloupe et de Martinique.**
(Illustrated flora of the phanerogams of Guadeloupe and Martinique.)
Jacques Fournet. Paris: Institut National de la Recherche
Agronomique, 1978. 1654p.

Although botanists do not yet consider the flora completely described, this is the most
comprehensive taxonomy of the phanerogams of Guadeloupe and Martinique. Listed
here are some 2,779 species divided into the following five groups: indigenous species; species that are now totally naturalized; subspontaneous species in the process of
being naturalized; species found only in a cultivated state; and species of uncertain
origins. Fournet lists 1,668 species as indigenous to the islands of Guadeloupe and
Martinique and links vernacular names to scientific nomenclature.

64 **Flore médicinale illustrée.** (Illustrated medicinal flora.)
Henri and Madeleine Stehlé. Pointe-À-Pitre, Guadeloupe: Anibal
Lautrec, 1962. vol. IX, *Flore Agronomique des Antilles Françaises.*
184p.

Some seventy-five of the most commonly encountered medicinal plants of the French
Antilles are listed in this useful volume. Plants are arranged by use ranging from such
categories as anti-asthmatics and anti-scorbutics to diuretics, stimulants, and vulne-
raires. Each entry is completely described and illustrated; related species are given.
Specific medicinal properties, ecology, and locations on Martinique and Guadeloupe
where the species can be found are provided.

65 **A general catalog of the birds noted from the islands of the Lesser
Antilles, &c.**
George N. Lawrence. *Smithsonian Miscellaneous Collections*, vol. 19
(1880), p. 486-88.

This article is a checklist of 128 species of birds found in the Lesser Antilles, given by
their scientific names. Distribution for each species is noted for Martinique, six other
Antillean islands, and the United States. This list will be useful for the birdwatcher
and professional ornithologist.

66 **Martinique revisited. The changing plant geographies of a West
Indian island.**
Clarissa Thérèse Kimber. College Station, Texas: Texas A & M Press,
1988. 458p. bibliog. maps.

This is a wonderfully illustrated historical plant geography of Martinique, which documents changes in the vegetational landscape during the last 350 years. The first two
chapters, one of which describes the physical environment of the island and another
which treats flora and vegetation, constitute perhaps the best extant geographical survey of Martinique. While the author describes her methodology as eclectic, she has
used an impressive array of archaeological, biological, and historical literature to complement her own extensive field work. The heart of the work is organized around
critical periods in French Caribbean history. Each of these six historical chapters contains a section on social and economic developments and another on changes in island
plant geography. The volume is also useful for its extensive bibliography and for its
appendices: one provides a systematic list of all plant species mentioned in the text;
another gives vernacular plant names and their scientific counterparts; and a final

appendix describes quality timbers from Martinique forests. This is a seminal study with many original maps and photographs.

67 The natural vegetation of the Windward & Leeward Islands.
John Stewart Beard.   Oxford: Clarendon Press, 1949. 192p. bibliog. maps.

The standard reference work for regional plant geography in the Windward and Leeward Islands, this volume treats physical and cultural factors that influence plant distributions. Beard also classifies and describes Antillean plant communities. The section on Martinique (p. 167-71) discusses primary and secondary rain forest, montane thickets, palm brakes, elfin woodland, seasonal forests, and dry scrub woodlands. A final section of the book compares Antillean vegetation with that of Trinidad and Tobago, Puerto Rico, and Mauritius.

68 The vegetation of the Antilles.
Richard A. Howard.   In: *Vegetation and vegetational history of northern Latin America*.   Edited by Alan Graham.   Amsterdam; London; New York: Elsevier Scientific Publishing Company, 1973. p. 1-37.

In this chapter Howard offers a biogeographical typology of West Indian plant genera associated with coastal, lowland, and montane formations. He also looks at the origins, relationships, and distributions of the vegetation of the Antilles, providing tables and maps of specific distributional patterns. The abundant examples of endemism and disjunct distributions, always important characteristics of island biota, are discussed. To date, however, the native Caribbean flora, of which Martinique forms a contiguous island subregion, has not been monographically studied as a whole. This chapter represents a valuable contribution to our understanding of broad vegetational patterns throughout the Antilles and of the variation found on each island.

69 Volcanism and vegetation in the Lesser Antilles.
Richard A. Howard.   *Journal of the Arnold Arboretum*, vol. 3, no. 3 (1962), p. 279-314.

This article is a useful summary of literature on and field sites of eruptive and fumarolic volcanic activity throughout the Lesser Antilles, including Martinique. Howard, who is a botanist, describes the impact of various types of volcanism on local vegetation. The article provides lists of species associated with particular microenvironments near new and active fumaroles, for which the author provides soil temperature and pH measurements. He describes the re-establishment of species in devastated areas by altitude and type of volcanism and then compares the Lesser Antillean situation to similarly studied volcanic islands such as Indonesia.

Travel Guides and
Tourism

70 **The Caribbean islands.**
   Thomas D. Boswell, Dennis Conway.   New Brunswick, New Jersey:
   Rutgers University Press, 1992. 242p.
Two university geographers wrote this guidebook for a ten-day tour of twelve
Caribbean islands. Day seven is spent on Martinique. A great deal of diverse information and original interpretation makes this a useful travel resource. The six-page
general introduction to the volume is an excellent overview of Caribbean climatic patterns, history, agricultural and economic geography, population patterns, house types,
and land forms. This book does not contain lodging or restaurant information but
would be excellent for cruise passengers or as a companion resource for the more
standard guidebooks.

71 **A cruising guide to the Caribbean.**
   William T. Stone, Anne M. Hays.   New York: G. P. Putnam's Sons,
   1991. 542p.
This general cruising guide covers the entire Caribbean; while it contains many anec-
dotes from the first author's twenty-five years of sailing experience in the region, it
contains only six pages devoted to Martinique. Its information on non-sailing subjects
such as culture, biology, and geology is superficial.

72 **Fielding's Caribbean 1993.**
   Margaret Zellers.   New York: Fielding Travel Books, 1993. 928p.
This guidebook contains a wide selection of low-cost lodgings, inns, and resort hotels
as well as standard tourist information. The short commentary on sites and attractions
is good but provides little historical, cultural, or geographical information.

73 **Fodor's Caribbean 93.**
New York; Toronto; London; Sydney; Aukland: Fodor's Travel
Publications, 1992. 692p.

Some thirty pages of the 1993 edition are devoted to Martinique. Most of the information is standard tourist fare, with few original or insightful offerings.

74 **A historical guide to Saint Pierre.**
Marie Chomereau-Lamotte.   Fort-de-France: Conseil Regional de la
Martinique, 1987. 96p.

This historical guide, which is richly illustrated with old photographs, drawings and maps, serves two purposes: it is a guidebook for the cosmopolitan, commercial city destroyed by volcanic eruption in 1902; and it is a resource to help obtain world heritage site designation for St. Pierre from the United Nations (UNESCO).

75 **Le developpement du tourisme à la Martinique.** (Tourism
development in Martinique.)
Georges Cazes.   *Cahiers d'Outre-Mer*, vol. 21, no. 83 (1968),
p. 225-56.

When this article was published, Martinique's tourist industry was noticeably undeveloped, especially when compared to islands such as Puerto Rico, Jamaica, and Barbados. Martinique lacked much hotel room capacity and any large resort hotels. The article rather systematically looks at patterns of growth in Caribbean tourism during the 1960s, with the object of better planning for similar growth and development on Martinique. This article is a good example of the kind of extrapolation that assumes larger airports, more hotels, and greater tourism are inexhaustible and highly desirable sources of revenue and development for Caribbean economies. It does not, however, consider tourism's effect on the local environment, income distribution, or culture.

Prehistory and Archaeology

76 **The analysis of the vertebrate fauna from the Macabou Site, Area F, Martinique.**
Linda J. Fraser.   *Boletin del Museo del Hombre Dominicano*, vol. 10, no. 16 (1981), p. 49-54.

This paper is a summary analysis of vertebrate faunal material excavated by Louis Allaire at the Macabou Site in southeast Martinique. It utilizes minimal numbers of individuals by age and size differences and duplicated skeletal elements to determine relative numbers by habitat. The author compares the Macabou material with sites from St. Lucia, Grenada, and Barbados, and concludes that it has the most similarities with St. Lucia; both showed a reliance on pelagic and offshore fishes, but utilized land mammals and sea turtles as well. Food sources were drawn almost equally from five distinct habitats on both Martinique and St. Lucia, demonstrating a diverse diet.

77 **The archeological problem in Martinique: a general view.**
Robert F. Pinchon.   In: *Proceedings of the First International Convention for the Study of pre-Columbian Culture in the Lesser Antilles.*   Fort-de-France: Société d'histoire de la Martinique, 1963. p. 75-80.

Two pottery manufacturing techniques on Martinique are distinguished in this article. One is what the author calls the 'three-stuck-parts' or moulded technique and the second is the simpler process known as the coiling technique. Pinchon speculates on whether the second is a degenerated form of the first and on whether or not either pottery type can be attributed to a specific linguistic group.

78 **L'art des Arawak et des Caraïbes des Petites Antilles, analyse de la décoration des céramiques.** (Arawak and Carib art in the Lesser Antilles. Analysis of ceramic decoration.)
Henry Petitjean Roget. *Les Cahiers du Ceraq (Centre d'études régionales Antilles-Guyane)*, no. 35, 1978, 60p. illus.

This volume is a descriptive analysis of decorative techniques and designs on pre-Columbian pottery in Martinique. The frog and the bat are the most common animal figures adorning pots. The paper discusses other frequently utilized designs and stylistic patterns and the text is complemented by 105 pages of illustrations.

79 **Caribbean.**
Irving Rouse, Louis Allaire. In: *Chronologies in New World Archaeology.* Edited by R. E. Taylor, Clement W. Meighan. New York: Academic Press, 1978. p. 431-81.

This chapter is an updating of the state of archaeology in the eastern half of the Caribbean in 1978. It presents dates and successions of native American peoples and complexes in six Eastern Caribbean regions prior to the European invasion of 1492. One of these regions is the Lesser Antilles, of which sites and ceramic complexes on Martinique form a major part of the discussion. This is a valuable reference work, both for an overall regional context and for any study focusing on prehistory and archaeology on Martinique.

80 **Collections archéologiques martiniquaises du Musée de l'Homme.** (Martinican archaeological collections in the Musée de l'Homme.)
Raoul d'Harcourt. *Journal de la Société des Américanistes*, nouvelle serie, vol. 41 (1952), p. 353-82.

The author describes the objects from excavations at the Sainte-Marie, La Salle site on Martinique contained in Collection 44-16 at the Musée de l'Homme. A later collection contains items from Paquemar, l'Espérance, and Marigot, which were excavated in 1949. Each collection is comprised of more than 1,000 pieces. Ceramics and rock and stone objects are shown on nine accompanying plates.

81 **Communication sur les petroglyphes de la Martinique.** (Communication on the petroglyphs of Martinique.)
Mario Mattioni. In: *Proceedings of the Fourth International Congress for the Study of pre-Columbian Cultures of the Lesser Antilles, Reduit Beach, St. Lucia, July 26-30, 1971.* Castries, St. Lucia: St. Lucia Archaeological and Historical Society, 1973. p. 25-32.

A rock containing eleven figures was discovered in southern Martinique in 1970. The author isolates each figure and compares it with petroglyphs from other Caribbean islands and Venezuela. The similarity in representations of the human body merits attention. Mattioni points out that potting was generally the work of women; in comparing the rock drawings with pottery designs, he also notes that the anthropomorphic figurations are quite similar. He proposes that the petroglyphs from various Caribbean islands emanate from the same cultural group and speculates about the possible use of similar religious symbols on both rocks and ceramics.

82 **Contribution à l'archéologie de la Martinique: le gisement de l'anse-Belleville.** (Contribution to the archaeology of Martinique: the Belleville cove site.)
Henri Reichlen, Paule Barret. *Journal de la société des Américanistes,* nouvelle série, vol. 32 (1940), p. 227-74.

This paper reports on the collection excavated by Revert in 1939 at l'Anse Belleville site near Prêcheur in the north of Martinique. After a description of the site's topography and stratigraphy, the article discusses excavated stone objects, including pestles and mortars, and bone objects. The ceramics described are pieces of bowls, plates, pots, jars, and both anthropomorphic and zoomorphic figurines. Finally, it treats the remains of a kitchen and the bones of small terrestrial and marine animals. This is one of the earliest reports of a Martinican archaeological site and is purely descriptive with no analysis.

83 **Contribution à l'archéologie de la Martinique. Le gisement du Paquemar.** (Contribution to Martinican archaeology. The Paquemar site.)
Henri Reichlen, Paule Barret. *Journal de la Société des Américanistes,* nouvelle série, vol. 33 (1941), p. 91-117.

A number of stone tools, shell implements, and ceramic fragments excavated from Paquemar in 1938 are described in this article. The ceramic pieces include polychrome sherds, bas-relief zoomorphic and anthropomorphic figures, engraved fragments, handles, necks, and disks. This is one of the earliest archaeological papers on Martinique, but is a purely descriptive piece. The collection is at the Musée de l'Homme in Paris.

84 **Early man in the West Indies.**
José M. Cruxent, Irving Rouse. *Scientific American,* vol. 221, no. 5 (1969), p. 42-52.

This article is a summary of knowledge about native American peopling of the West Indies in 1969. The authors argue for a much earlier date (7,000 years before present) than that generally accepted (2,000 years before present) at the time the article was written. Although the work centres on Hispaniola, its hypotheses are clearly relevant to the developing literature on prehistoric Martinique.

85 **Essai sur les concordances archéologiques du Venezuela à la Martinique.** (Essay on the archaeological similarities between Venezuela and Martinique.)
Mario Mattioni. In: *Proceedings of the Fifth International Congress for the Study of pre-Columbian Cultures of the Lesser Antilles, Antigua, July 22-29, 1973.* Antigua: Antigua National Trust, Antigua Archaeological Society, 1974, p. 21-27.

Decorative ceramic motifs from Martinique are compared with those from Venezuela in this study. Mattioni tries to arrive at some working hypotheses involving techniques, their diffusion, and change. He proposes that various groups of people were regularly moving in the Lesser Antilles and that each of these groups had a singular cultural evolution. Therefore the archaeologist finds in certain beds and strata isolated types that represent stratigraphic aberrations and unique influences. Mattioni applies these hypotheses to Saladoid complexes of Venezuela and Martinique, the latter at Vivé, Diamant, and Fond Brûle. He then proposes a looser, more complex interpretation of cultural evolution and relationships than found in earlier papers on Martinican archaeology. Previously there had been an almost universal attempt to attribute a succession of techniques and sites to proto-Arawakan, Arawakan, and/or Carib peoples. This is a more fluid, creative interpretation.

86   **Essai de taxonomie des ensembles reconstitués.** (Essay on a taxonomy of reconstructed ensembles.)
       Jacques Petitjean-Roget.   In: *Proceedings of the Third International Congress for the Study of pre-Columbian Cultures of the Lesser Antilles, St. George's, Grenada, July 7-11, 1969*, p. 8-14.

This paper establishes a method to analyse the morphology of a ceramic ensemble and therefore to classify it and differentiate it from other ensembles. This taxonomy is to facilitate the study of the several distinct horizons represented in the many archaeological sites on Martinique.

87   **Étude comparative des tessons gravés ou incisés.** (Comparative study of engraved or incised sherds.)
       Jacques Petitjean-Roget, Henry Petitjean-Roget.   In: *Proceedings of the Fourth International Congress for the Study of pre-Columbian Cultures of the Lesser Antilles, Reduit Beach, St. Lucia, July 26-30, 1971.*   Castries, St. Lucia: St Lucia Archaeological and Historical Society, 1973. p. 157-73.

This paper is a comparative study of 120 engraved sherds and 85 incised sherds from various Martinican archaeological sites. Engraving is abundant in the earliest horizon (250 AD), rare in the second (450 AD), and disappears completely in the third (1000 AD). Incising is rare in the first, flourishes chiefly in the second, and is still widely represented in the third. The authors compare many traits of the two ceramic types and the article is copiously illustrated with plates.

88   **Étude des ensembles reconstitués de la Martinique.** (Study of reconstructed ensembles in Martinique.)
       Jacques Petitjean-Roget.   In: *Proceedings of the Third International Congress for the Study of pre-Columbian Cultures of the Lesser Antilles, St.George's, Grenada, July 7-11, 1969.* p. 15-27.

A statistical method is used in this paper to analyse and categorize the structure of reconstructed ceramic ensembles on Martinique. The author recognizes three distinct cultural horizons on the island which he labels 'Carib', 'Arawak', and 'proto-Arawak'. To each he applies a two-part taxonomy based first on such shape characteristics as diameter, size, thickness, rim, and height; and second, on design and decorative elements. After combining the two he proposes that specific types of pottery characterize each horizon and that styles are most different between Horizon I and Horizon III.

89   Étude des pates céramiques de la Martinique pre-colombienne.
(Study of ceramic pastes in pre-Columbian Martinique.)
Jeanne Gauthier.   In: *Proceedings of the Fifth International Congress
for the Study of Pre-Columbian Cultures of the Lesser Antilles, Antigua,
July 22-28, 1973*.   Antigua: Antigua National Trust, Antigua
Archaeological Society, 1974, p. 133-39.
Gauthier examines the pastes of twenty-eight sherds from eight sites representing
three successive occupations on Martinique. The author found northern ceramics to
differ from those of the southern part of the island in both technique and material. She
attributes the great difference in volcanic glasses in the sherds to explosive activity
during the prehistoric period in the area around Mont Pelée in the north.

90   Étude des Tessons. (Study of Sherds.)
Jacques Petitjean-Roget.   In: *Proceedings of the Third International
Congress for the Study of pre-Columbian Cultures of the Lesser
Antilles, St. George's, Grenada, July 7-11, 1969*.   Grenada: Grenada
National Museum. p. 87-94.
This paper proposes a systematic method of studying Martinican ceramic sherds. It
begins with an analysis of the substance of which the sherd is made and how it has
been utilized and transformed. This is followed by a study of the sherd itself and the
techniques and features that give it an identity and particular appearance, including
colour, designs, incised features, engraved features, and relief motifs. Study then
focuses on the sherd as a pottery fragment in a particular site: form may show the
fragment's function as a handle, neck, lug or other part of a larger piece when all are
studied together. Finally, there is analysis of the sherd as part of an already defined
pottery type or style. The author then utilizes this method to analyse sherds from the
Fond Brûle and Diamant sites on Martinique.

91   Étude d'un horizon Arawak et proto-Arawak à la Martinique à
partir du niveau II du Diamant. (Study of an Arawak and
proto-Arawak horizon from level II of Diamant in Martinique.)
Jacques Petitjean-Roget.   In: *Proceedings of the Second International
Congress for the Study of pre-Columbian Cultures of the Lesser
Antilles*.   St. Ann's Garrison, Barbados: Barbados Museum, 1968,
p. 61-68.
This brief paper describes sherds and types of pottery from level II of Diamant, and
compares them with ceramics from horizon I of Diamant and other sites on Martinique
as well as other islands of the Lesser Antilles. Widespread in this horizon are composite vessels, circular deep dishes with handles and wide borders, and a bottle type
called 'scent burners', with quite narrow mouths. Petitjean-Roget also discusses
incising, decorations, and paints.

92 **Étude d'un horizon Caraïbe à la Martinique à partir de niveau III du Diamant.** (Study of a Carib horizon from level III of Diamant in Martinique.)
Jacques Petitjean-Roget. In: *Proceedings of the Second International Congress for the Study of pre-Columbian Cultures in the Lesser Antilles.* St. Ann's Garrison, Barbados: Barbados Museum, 1968, p. 125-33.

Petitjean-Roget characterizes the differences in pottery surfaces and pottery-making techniques among the three levels at Diamant. He observes the decline in painted sherds from the third to second levels, and from the second to the first, or most recent level. Decoration of sherds practically disappears in the upper layer. He provides a diagrammatic distribution of rim shapes and plate style by horizon and by beds within horizons. From radio-carbon dating, and the relative abundance of plates in each bed, Petitjean-Roget dates the earliest ceramic-making peoples as arriving on Martinique about 250 AD, reaching their peak numbers by about 800 AD, and experiencing a perturbation that reduced their numbers by half between 1000 and 1100 AD. He links this decline with the concurrent appearance of 'footed plates,' which he relates to Island Caribs.

93 **Les grandes familles des formes du 'Saladoide insulaire' au site de Vivé à la Martinique.** (The major families of 'Island Saladoid' forms at the Vivé site on Martinique.)
Mario Mattioni. In: *Proceedings of the Sixth International Congress for the Study of pre-Columbian Cultures of the Lesser Antilles. Point À Pitre, Guadeloupe, July 6-12, 1975.* Gainesville, Florida: Florida State Museum, University of Florida, 1976. p. 11-14.

Mattioni lists and describes the nine ceramic types that form the overwhelming majority of Saladoid vessels excavated at the Vivé site on Martinique. Some seventy per cent of all sherds derive from cooking pots. The rest come from manioc platters or griddles, engraved bowls, bowls decorated in bas-relief on sepia, bowls, scent burners, bottles, bowls in red wash, and jars. This is a concise, well-illustrated, and well-defined typology. The article additionally conveys the relative percentages of each ceramic type represented in the entire ceramic ensemble.

94 **Introduction à l'archéologie martiniquaise.** (Introduction to Martinican archaeology.)
Robert Pinchon. *Journal de la Société des Américanistes,* vol. 41, nouvelle série (1952), p. 305-52.

Pinchon, who began archaeological work on Martinique in 1945, in this article sets out the sites and artifacts associated with Arawak and Carib presence on the island. Forty sites, all located near the Atlantic east coast of the island, are reviewed. Arawak sites are found on the northeast coast, on small floodplains near the ocean; Marigot is the most important Arawak site with the best ceramic pieces. Carib sites, dating from the 11th century, are all along the Atlantic on both plains and plateau areas, with Paquemar the most typical. Carib artifacts do not attain the artistry of Arawakan pieces. Pinchon proposes that ceramic techniques clearly differentiate the two groups and that the Caribs are more sea-oriented with huge shell-heaps of lambi and other molluscs. He presents a summary of ceramic techniques, stating that Carib is not a degenerative tradition of the Arawak, but a totally different tradition. He reviews Rouse's earlier work on pre-Columbian migration and movement and relates them to Martinique. Pinchon's proposals remained intact until the work of Louis Allaire twenty-five years later.

95 **Lowland South America and the Antilles.**

Betty J. Meggars, Clifford Evans. In: *Ancient native America.* Edited by Jesse D. Jennings. San Francisco: W. H. Freeman & Co., 1978. p. 543-92.

Meggars and Evans present an original hypothesis and synthesis on the origins and dispersals of prehistoric native Americans. This article places the Antilles within a context of peoples and environments east of the Andes and the Central American mainland. Using a biogeographical approach, the authors reconstruct a chronological comparison of culture groups and movements of peoples. The first dated pottery made in the Lesser Antilles appears early in the Common Era and belongs to the Saladoid tradition, apparently spreading to the islands from Trinidad. Whether these ceramic-making peoples replaced or coexisted with earlier, non-pottery producing inhabitants is as yet unknown.

96 **Macabu [sic] excavations, Martinique, 1972-79.**

Louis Allaire. *Boletin del Museo del Hombre Dominicano*, vol. 10, no. 16 (1981), p. 41-48.

This paper reports on excavations of a large Suazoid series settlement at Macabou on the southeast coast of Martinique. The author establishes three Suazoid phases spanning 1100-1400 AD. The first is a widely-distributed pottery with finely indented rims and Caliviny linear painting. The second is later and lacks the finger-indented rims and linear painting, shows greater emphasis on plain ware, and displays inspiration from Chicoid cultures of the Lesser Antilles. The third assemblage now seems aberrant and cannot clearly be assigned. None of these phases, however, can be attributed to historic island Caribs, nor are any Suazoid components from the historic period. The role of Suazoid peoples in the ethnic and linguistic history of Martinique is still in doubt.

97 **On the historicity of Carib migrations in the Lesser Antilles.**

Louis Allaire. *American Antiquity*, vol. 45, no. 2 (1980), p. 238-45.

Allaire, whose archaeological work was conducted on Martinique, here sheds new light on long-accepted interpretations of Carib origins and expansion in the Lesser Antilles. His paper effectively challenges and re-examines interpretations of all previous ethnohistorical and archaeological data regarding Arawak and Carib identity, interaction, and movements in Martinique, the Lesser Antilles, and the Guianas. This is an important paper, relevant to all earlier archaeological work on Martinique.

Prehistory and Archaeology

98 **L'outillage lithique d'un site du nord-est de la Martinique.** (Stone implements from a site in northeast Martinique.)
Mario Mattioni. In: *Proceedings of the Fourth International Congress for the Study of pre-Columbian Cultures of the Lesser Antilles. Reduit Beach, St. Lucia, July 26-30, 1971.* Castries, St. Lucia: St. Lucia Archaeological and Historical Society, 1973. p. 84-89.
This paper examines stone tools from the Vivé site on the northeast coast of Martinique. Mortars, graters, axes, and polishers were among the many tools brought to the surface in 1970 in the course of a preliminary dig. The site had not been disturbed and these stone tools, found in two distinct beds, represent an ensemble of Arawak rock objects. There is little difference between the materials in the two, completely separated beds. The tools are finely elaborated and not very numerous. The article contains drawings of the tools as they were found in the site as well as drawings of the most characteristic forms.

99 **Paquemar revisited.**
Louis Allaire. In: *Proceedings of the Fifth International Congress for the Study of pre-Columbian Cultures of the Lesser Antilles, Antigua, July 22-28, 1973.* Antigua: Antigua National Trust, Antigua Archaeological Society, 1974. p. 117-26.
This article reports on Allaire's work at Paquemar on Martinique to re-examine earlier interpretations of the site. The paper provides data from stratigraphic tests of pits at five different middens. Allaire concludes that several occupational sites are represented as well as two major complexes covering a period from about 500 AD to the end of the prehistoric era. Significantly, he found no complexes that could be attributed to historic island Carib groups and he therefore concludes that the use of Paquemar as a late Carib complex should be abandoned.

100 **Pattern and process in West Indian archaeology.**
Irving Rouse. *World Archaeology*, vol. 91, no. 1 (1977), p. 1-11.
Rouse classifies archaeological research by the deductions it permits about prehistoric cultures. He considers simple collection and classification the first level of study; making inferences about the societies producing the artifacts is the second level; hypotheses on the cultural systems and their environmental relationships are a third level; and producing theories of social and cultural-ecological change are a fourth level of study and interpretation. Archaeological research in the West Indies has only recently begun to involve third- and fourth-level interpretations. This article is an important review of archaeological studies in the West Indies.

101 **Prehistory of the West Indies.**
Irving Rouse. *Science*, vol. 144, no. 3,618 (1964), p. 499-513.
The West Indies, because of their location in relation to several mainland regions, have generated a range of hypotheses about their peopling. Here Rouse describes the physical environment, the basic characteristics of Amerindian cultures, and dates and successions of peoples in the islands. Rouse's work became the standard interpretation into which later studies of Martinique were fitted. An authority on Arawakan and Carib peoples, Rouse argues for movements from the South American mainland north through the Lesser Antilles.

102 **Recherche d'une méthode pour l'étude de la décoration des céramiques pré-colombiennes de la Martinique.** (Search for a method to study pre-Columbian ceramic decoration in Martinique.) Jacques Petitjean-Roget, Henry Petitjean-Roget. In: *Proceedings of the Fourth International Congress for the Study of pre-Columbian Cultures of the Lesser Antilles. Reduit Beach, St. Lucia, July 26-30, 1971.* Castries, St. Lucia: St. Lucia Archaeological and Historical Society, 1973. p. 151-56.

The authors discuss decoration, form, and function in ceramics. They propose to examine elementary motifs in techniques, form, and function and at different levels (sherds and vessels for example). One can verify the existence of ensembles formed by a collection of motifs repeated in a certain manner on the same vessel or from one vessel to another. They term this 'themes'. 'Decoration' is the total decorative ensemble on a vessel and is the study of relations between themes. The archaeologist looks for internal laws in a system of decoration and to differentiate one system from another and ultimately to interpret how one succeeds another.

103 **Recherches précolombiennes à la Martinique.** (Pre-Columbian research in Martinique.) Jacques Petitjean-Roget. *Actes de la Société de Américanistes*, vol. 55, no. 2 (1966).

This is a report on the history of archaeological work on Martinique, the organized study of which dates only from the late 1930s. The author reports on the difficulty of separating Carib and Arawak sherds in the sites, but here details a method and carbon 14 dates which confirm styles and dates from approximately 180 AD and 475 AD.

104 **Salvage excavations at the Fond-Brûle Site, Martinique. Final Report.** Mario Mattioni, translated, edited, and with a foreword by Louis Allaire. *University of Manitoba Anthropology Papers*, no. 27, 1982. 25p. illus. maps.

This paper reports on the prehistoric Fond-Brûle settlement on the northeast coast of Martinique. Mattioni considers the site a classic example of early Saladoid settlement: it is situated alongside a stream for access to fresh water, close to the sea for fishing and transportation, and near agricultural land for manioc cultivation. More than 11,000 sherds were recovered and analysed, but what distinguishes this work are the sherd distribution charts for a wide surface area and the maps of hearth remains that permit an idea of residential settlement and activity patterns. The site carries a radiocarbon date of 130 AD.

105 **Salvage excavations at the Vivé Site, Martinique. Final Report.** Mario Mattioni, translated, edited, and with a foreword by Louis Allaire. *University of Manitoba Anthropology Papers*, no. 23, 1979. 56p. maps. plates.

When it was published this paper was considered the most extensive study of an early Saladoid series settlement in the Lesser Antilles. An eruption of Mont Pelée in the 3rd century AD preserved an occupation floor of hearths, fireplaces, and heavy grinding stones. The occupation is dated to 220 AD, includes a high density of potsherds and five burials, and covers some 100 square metres along the Capot River near the north-east coast of Martinique. The paper, an important one for archaeology in Martinique and the Lesser Antilles, includes a reconstruction of a portion of a 2nd century village in Martinique based on inferences from ceramics and post moulds.

106   **La 'Savane des Pétrifications' (Martinique); un gisement de l'âge lithique?** (The 'Savannah of Petrifications' [Martinique]; a bed from the Stone Age?)
Henri Petitjean-Roget.   In: *Proceedings of the Fifth International Congress for the Study of pre-Columbian Cultures of the Lesser Antilles. Antigua, July 22-28, 1973.*   Antigua: Antigua National Trust, Antigua Archaeological Society, 1974. p. 82-93.

About 180 worked stone tools, the majority made of yellow jasper, were found at a preceramic site from Martinique near Pointe d'Enfer at the extreme south of the island in St. Anne commune. Because all the ceramic archaeological sites contain jasper and no ceramics have been found anywhere near the rock savannah, the author has assigned an earlier date to it. The paper also includes a classification of the objects and a diagrammatic representation of their position on the savannah. Photographs of four-teen specimens accompany the article. New data from Trinidad and Antigua, along with this from Martinique, raise the question of dates and origins of lithic age popula-tions in the Lesser Antillean arc.

107   **Symbolisme de la décoration des poteries Arawak.** (Symbolism of the decoration on Arawak ceramics.)
Mario Mattioni.   In: *Proceedings of the Second International Congress for the Study of pre-Columbian Cultures of the Lesser Antilles.*   St. Ann's Garrison, Barbados: Barbados Museum, 1968. p. 69-80.

Mattioni reports here on ten excavations at the Diamant Site on Martinique. He presents a profile of the terrain to a depth of 120 centimetres, describing the soil and abundance of sherds for each of six distinct layers. Two layers are especially rich in sherds and are separated by ten centimetres of soil that contain very few ceramics; moreover, the pottery in both layers is coiled with joined pieces. Mattioni believes, due to decoration and construction style, that both are Arawak. Instead of attributing the separated beds to two different peoples, as was previously common, he proposes that a natural disaster like a volcanic eruption could have made the site uninhabitable for a period, with descendants of the previous inhabitants returning. At the Fond Brûle site, in the bourg of Lorrain, Mattioni found only one archaeological layer, abruptly ending at between eighty and ninety centimetres. In decoration, form, and profile, the pottery is similar to that at Diamant, although the glaze at Diamant is thicker. Mattioni devises two schemes, one by profile and shape, the other by decorative motifs, to see if certain forms and decorative characteristics correspond. He then comments on the ritual and ceremonial elements he finds in the examined ceramics.

108 **Les thèmes de décoration de la poterie Arawak.** (Decoration themes on Arawak pottery.)
J. P. Duprat.   In: *Proceedings of the Fifth International Congress for the Study of pre-Columbian Cultures of the Lesser Antilles, Antigua, July 22-28, 1973.*   Antigua: Antigua National Trust, Antigua Archaeological Society, 1974, p. 72-81.

This paper subjects Arawak pottery from the Sainte-Marie site on Martinique to an analysis of decoration motifs. Engraved decorations applied after baking are totally geometrical and include curved and straight lines and grills. Engraving applied before baking is done on a paint. Paint decoration is present on most pottery, the great majority with the rims or interior in red. There are also polychrome vessels, with red, white, and orange the most used colours. Shapes used in the pottery include anthropomorphic and zoomorphic figures. Line drawings illustrating each design category accompany the article.

Mt. Pelée and the island population of Martinique.
See item no. 50.

History

Regional and general

109 The African exchange: toward a biological history of black people.
Edited by Kenneth F. Kiple. Durham, North Carolina: Duke
University Press, 1987. 280p. bibliog.

This edited volume is composed of original and timely scholarly essays on the morbidity and mortality of African-American populations. It covers the health status and hunger of slave populations in the 1800s as well as present-day diseases such as hypertension among black Americans. The opening essay surveys the recent literature on all aspects of blacks' biological past and is a good starting point for any health-related historical or contemporary study of a black population. There are many references to West Indian populations.

110 The Atlantic slave trade: a census.
Philip D. Curtin. Madison, Milwaukee; London: University of
Wisconsin Press, 1969. 338p. bibliog.

Curtin has produced the definitive work on the magnitude, movements, and segments of the colonial Atlantic slave trade. It is an ambitious volume that surpasses and integrates all previous work on the overall slave trade, its spatial, historical, and political components, and temporal trends. One chapter on the French slave trade of the 18th century is based on documents from Nantes, the principal French slave trading port. Martinique is separated out in most reported categories, which include ethnic origins, estimated slave numbers, and slave population growth rates.

111 The Caribbean slave, a biological history.
Kenneth F. Kiple. Cambridge, England; London; New York; New
Rochelle; Melbourne; Sydney: Cambridge University Press, 1984.

Drawn from demographic, nutritional, biological, and medical sources, this interdisciplinary history is a seminal contribution to the growing literature on the epidemiology, morbidity, and mortality of Caribbean black populations. The first section on background and biology treats the harsh West African environment and the genetic selection it wrought on survivors. Section two looks at the nutrition, malnutrition, demography, and mortality of slave populations in the West Indies. The final section on pathogens and politics examines the relationship between tropical diseases, white settlement in the Caribbean, enslavement, and racism. Kiple discusses how the very factors that allowed African-Americans to survive in the past have contributed to the rapid population growth in the present-day Caribbean. Although Martinique is only mentioned a few times in the text, the entire volume is an essential reference for any study of island demographics and population history and biology.

112 **A family of islands.**
Alec Waugh.   Garden City, New York: Doubleday & Co., 1964. 348p.
This is a light journalistic history of the West Indies from 1492 until 1898. It is a quite readable overview for the entire region, and Martinique is mentioned numerous times. It suffers, however, from being among the many superficial treatments of the Caribbean, and emphasizes European political and economic interests there. The more serious reader will want to consult more balanced studies.

113 **The French in the West Indies.**
W. Adolphe Roberts.   New York: Cooper Square Publishers, 1971. 335p.
Originally published in 1942, this is a broad, general history of the French presence in the Caribbean and the evolution of a creole society there from the 17th century until 1941. Although the author uses standard historical accounts, this is not a scholarly work. There are numerous references to Martinique and Martinicans.

114 **The French struggle for the West Indies, 1665-1713.**
Nellis M. Crouse.   New York: Columbia University Press, 1943. 324p.
This narrative covers the many battles and wars fought in the French West Indies between 1666 and 1713, primarily between French and English forces, and ending with the Treaty of Utrecht. Although the focus is in the West Indies, the action is totally a reflection of European empire building. The author believes that the constant military activity prevented colonists from achieving the economic prosperity they realized in the period after 1713. While governors and troops in the French West Indies are mentioned, this account is not much concerned with life in the islands. It is, however, an excellent political and military overview.

115 **The French West Indies: a socio-historical interpretation.**
René V. Achéen, F. R. Rifaux.   In: *Contemporary Caribbean: a sociological reader.*   Edited by Susan Craig.   Trinidad and Tobago: published by the author and printed at the College Press, 1981-82. vol. 1/2, p. 191-212.
Political-economic trends and social tensions during three periods are examined: the years between 1650 and 1848, which saw the rise of sugar monoculture, the downfall of small white farmers, the increase in black populations and the slave rebellions that led to the abolition of slavery; the period 1848-1948, which witnessed *Béké* (white creole) investment in island mills, the rise of a black peasantry and petty bourgeoisie

to political but not social or economic equality; and from departmentalization in 1948 to the present, which has been characterized by the accentuation of the French economic hold on the islands and the growth of a subsidized administrative sector. Achéen and Rifaux connect the present noncompetitive nature of island agriculture, low upward social mobility, and high unemployment with island class struggles, rivalry between the metropolis and the overseas departments, and opposing social forces in the islands.

116 **Histoire économique de la Guadeloupe et de la Martinique du XVIIe siècle à nos jours.** (Economic history of Guadeloupe and Martinique from the 17th century to the present.)
   Alain-Philippe Blérald. Paris: Éditions Karthala, 1986. 336p.

This volume is a historical political economy that analyses developments in Martinique and Guadeloupe since the islands were first bound to France and Europe in the early 17th century. The first section, focused on the pre-departmental period, examines slavery, the colonial *exclusif* and protectionist policies, the establishment of capitalist production, and the concentration of money and the means of production. The second part, devoted to the contemporary period, considers aspects of post-war Antillean underdevelopment, particularly changes in island agricultural production and social transformations. Blérald concludes that multinational capital and the local oligarchy continue to reap the benefits of Martinican economic change, despite the vastly different role of the French government and private investment. The book frames island history in a world system perspective; its author is senior lecturer at the Université des Antilles-Guyane in Martinique.

117 **Histoire générale des Antilles.** (General history of the Antilles.)
   Adrien Dessalles. Paris: Libraire-Éditeur, 1847-48, 5 vols. vol. 1, 577p; vol. 2, 487p; vol. 3, 483p; vol. 4, 611p.

The author is a member of a distinguished Martinican family; his father and grandfather served as councillors on the Supreme Council. The present work consists of four parts in five volumes. Part one treats the establishment of France, England, and Spain in the islands up to 1665, the commercial *exclusif* each developed, and their illicit commerce with the Dutch. Part two examines the wars which have taken place in the Antilles and the establishment of a second French trading company and its revocation. Part three covers the period 1680-1711, the comings and goings of government officers, and the manoeuvrings of the English and French in the islands; it is primarily concerned with imperial politics and commerce. The final two parts constitute a legislative history, composed of the annals of the supreme council of Martinique from 1717 until 1774. Each volume is supplemented with official documents, such as: the names of property owners in Martinique in 1671; details of the general census of Martinique, Guadeloupe, and St. Christopher in 1701; the census of Martinique in 1713; a table on the conditions of negros introduced in Martinique between 1714 and 1721; and a list of merchants resident in Martinique in 1742 who obtained permission to buy boats in foreign islands.

118 **Histoire générale des Antilles habitées par les françois.** (General
history of the Antilles inhabited by the French.)
Jean Baptiste DuTertre. Paris: Thomas Jolly, 1667-71. vol. 1, 593p;
vol. 2, 539p; vol. 3, 325p; vol. 4, 362p. maps.
DuTertre, a French Dominican priest and missionary, travelled widely in the West
Indies and observed French, English, and Dutch colonists on the French islands. This
is an invaluable eyewitness account of the earliest religious and colonist activities, of
the native Americans, and of the first slaves in the French Antilles. Volume one deals
primarily with the establishment of French colonies on Martinique, Guadeloupe, and
St. Christopher. It also tells of Dutch inhabitants who, expelled from Brazil, took ref-
uge on Martinique and Guadeloupe. The second volume, a natural history, describes
island climate, rocks, plants, trees, cultivated plants, both subsistence and commercial
agriculture and processing, as well as fish, birds, and land animals. Probably the most
consulted sections in this volume, however, are DuTertre's accounts of the native
Americans and slaves. Volume three discusses property ownership, the establishment
of the Royal Company of the West Indies, and the governing of the islands until the
war between France and England in 1666. Volume four treats the period from 1666
until the Peace of Breda between France, England, and Holland in 1667, and is largely
an account of hostilities, repositioning, and the participation of native Americans in
battles.

119 **The history of sugar.**
Noel Deerr. London: Chapman & Hall, 1949. vol. 1, 258p; vol. 2,
636p.
This is an unsurpassed treatment of the history of sugarcane and the connection
between sugar and slavery. The first volume of the two-volume work systematically
follows sugarcane from its southeast Asian origins to its introduction across subtropical Asia and the Mediterranean to the American colonies of various European powers.
One chapter discusses the French colonies and contains numerous references to and
data on Martinican sugar production. Volume two considers the interrelationship of
sugar and slavery and includes chapters on alternative sources of labour after emancipation, policies and technologies affecting the sugar industry, and alternative
sources of sugar. This history, along with *The Caribbean sugar industries* by
G. B. Hagelberg, is the essential starting point for any study of the Martinican sugar
industry.

120 **The loss of El Dorado: a history.**
V. S. Naipaul. New York: Alfred A. Knopf, 1970. 394p. bibliog.
Useful for a background to the whole of the Caribbean, this book is a history of
Trinidad by the eminent novelist and essayist V. S. Naipaul, who was born and completed secondary school there. The narrative focuses on two events: the 16th-century
search for the elusive golden city of El Dorado, said to be located on the South
American continent; and the British capture of Trinidad in 1797 and the subsequent
establishment of a slave colony on the island. The volume is a broad portrait of the
activity of all the European powers in the Caribbean for the more than 200 years
between 1592 and 1813. Although various references are made to Martinique, the volume is most useful as one interpretation of the complex early Caribbean history of
which Martinique is a part.

121 **The negro in the French West Indies.**
Shelby T. McCoy. Lexington, Kentucky: University of Kentucky
Press, 1966. 278p.

This well-documented scholarly account is the best English source available which
focuses exclusively on the history of blacks in the French West Indies, including
Martinique. Its coverage is from the earliest days of the colonies until the 1960s, and
includes the Code Noir; the political, military, and economic lives of slaves; emancipation in the 1840s; post-emancipation black status and notable blacks from the
islands. This is an original and quite readable history for which many pertinent documents have been consulted; it will serve as a good general source for any historical
study of Martinique.

122 **Nouveau voyage aux isles de l'Amerique.** (New voyage to the
American islands.)
R. P. Labat. Fort-de-France, Martinique: Éditions des Horizons
Caraïbes, 1972. 4 vols.

This is a reissue of Father Labat's original account, published in 1732, of his twelve-
year stay in the French Antilles between 1693 and 1705. Much of his time was spent
on Martinique. This 1,600-page record in four volumes is not only an account of
Labat's activities, but also of the natural history of the islands, local government, cash
crops, and the island economy. The reader will find information on subjects ranging
from the processing of bitter manioc and the making of indigo, to descriptions of
native insects, fish, turtles, and mammals. The coverage extends further to sugar
estates, mill equipment, grades of sugar, slave complement and finances; and the slave
trade, island trade with Europe, and land concessions. For natural history and the
Columbian exchange this is a more useful work than that of DuTertre, the other
17th-century chronicler.

123 **Pirates and privateers of the Caribbean.**
Jenifer Marx. Malabar, Florida: Krieger Publishing Company, 1992.
310p.

A well-written history of piracy in the Caribbean, this is based on archival work in
depositories of most countries with past and present economic interests in the region.
The author traces changes in the nature and operation of Caribbean sea robberies, the
personalities involved, and how piracy changed from a largely court-sanctioned activity in the period before 1700 to independent, universally-outlawed acts of violence
thereafter. Marx shows how in the 16th and 17th centuries privateering was an extension of European imperialist policies. There are numerous references to Martinique,
which was the principal French privateer base during the colonial period and which
owes much of its early prosperity to privateering.

124 **La question nationale en Guadeloupe et en Martinique.** (The
national question in Guadeloupe and Martinique.)
Alain-Philippe Blérald. Paris: Éditions l'Harmattan, 1988. 211p.
bibliog.

This political history analyses three stages in Antillean development from the standpoint of changes and transformations in French political and economic policy. Despite
a change from mercantilism and slavery to democracy and capitalism and then to
departmentalization and assimilation, policies have always benefited the Martinican

oligarchy and resulted in a concentration of wealth and power. The highly polarized Antillean society continues to be so. Blérald scrutinizes the unsatisfactory and para-doxical situation of the French Antilles under the Mitterrand régime, with the latter's stand regarding decentralization of the overseas departments, and weighs the interests and effectiveness of departmentalist and anti-colonialist elements in island politics.

125   A short history of the West Indies.
J. H. Parry, Philip Sherlock.   London: MacMillan, 1971, 3rd edition. 337p. bibliog.

This volume is notable among histories of the Caribbean because it is the first that treats it as a geographical region with its own economic and social history worthy of study. The history begins with the European invasion of 1492 and, while it concen-trates on the British Caribbean, there are numerous references to the French West Indies and Martinique. The authors craft the Caribbean as a corridor through which passed peoples, goods, and policies, all imported from somewhere else and destined for someone else's profit. Each island has thus been more focused on Europe or the United States than on neighbouring islands or, indeed, itself. Despite this political and historical separateness, the authors weave together the parallel experiences of all the Caribbean islands to shape a uniquely regional interpretation.

126   Slavery and the plantation in the New World.
Sidney Greenfield.   *Journal of Inter-American Studies*, vol. 11 (Jan. 1969), p. 44-57.

Greenfield examines the difference in plantation systems and slavery established by Iberian peoples and by Anglo-Saxon peoples through looking at the re-establishment of the system from the Atlantic islands occupied by Portugal. He discusses how through time, Portuguese household organization, Dutch commercial know-how, and the later acquisition of larger properties by Anglo-Saxon nuclear families all contrib-uted to the establishment of distinctive American plantation systems. The article is a valuable historical framework into which the Martinique plantation may be fitted.

127   The sugar cane industry: an historical geography from its origins to 1914.
J. D. Galloway.   Cambridge, England: Cambridge University Press, 1989. 266p. bibliog. maps.

The diffusion and growth of the sugar cane industry is described in this book, from its Asian origins in cane-growing almost 3,000 years ago. Spreading from India to the Mediterranean region more than 1,000 years ago, land systems, labour systems, and technologies of sugar making gradually evolved into the forms that became wide-spread in the slave plantations of the American tropics from about 1550 to 1800. The 19th century brought innovations and changes in labour, finance, and processing tech-nology. In Martinique the central factory in the field was a comparatively early innovation for the Caribbean region (p. 155-58). There are many references to Martinique in this excellent work, which is the only modern, comprehensive history of the sugar industry in English.

Colonial period to emancipation in 1848

128 **Ambiguous revolution in the Caribbean: the white Jacobins, 1789-1800.**
Anne Perotin-Dumon. *Historical Reflections*, vol. 13, nos. 1-2 (1986). p. 499-515.

This is a well-reasoned article that looks at events in the Caribbean in relation to the French Revolution, with particular attention to the complex divisions between white creoles and metropolitans and between creole blacks and whites. The author distinguishes two revolutions: one against the colonial system and favouring total independence; the other against the agriculturally-oriented *ancién régime* and supporting a colonialist commercial republic. Haiti effected the former, while the Lesser Antilles aligned behind the latter and lost. After a growing freedom and prosperity based on inter-American trade during the 18th century, the Antilles returned to a life based on creole élites, property, slaves, and dependency in the 19th century. Perotin-Dumon concludes that the fleeting effects of the French Revolution are understandable given that its supporters, the white Jacobins, were first and foremost Europeans, equally dependent on the metropolis. She links the many paradoxes of French colonial policy, revolutions in the Western Hemisphere, and the French Revolution. This is an insightful article.

129 **The Bissette affair and the French colonial question.**
Melvin O. Kennedy. *The Journal of Negro History*, vol. 45, no. 1 (Jan. 1960), p. 1-10.

A minor slave revolt on Martinique in 1822 incited fears among the planter aristocracy that the slave population, led by freed negroes, was about to overwhelm them. This led to a ruthless repression – the arrest of most freedmen, the confiscation of their property, and their deportation from the island. Bissette, a wealthy black merchant, was sentenced to life imprisonment in France, where he caught the attention of a young liberal lawyer who championed his cause and, ultimately, the abolition of slavery. This article is a detailed account of the role this *cause célèbre* played in bringing about an awareness of the need for complete reform in French colonial policy.

130 **British way, French way: opinion building and revolution in the second French slave emancipation.**
Seymour Drescher. *American Historical Review*, vol. 96, no. 3 (1991). p. 709-34.

This is a well-documented examination of both French slave emancipations: the first, in 1794, which lasted only until the Treaty of Amiens in 1802; and the second, in 1848, which endured. Drescher argues that emancipation at mid-century was an inevitable outcome of the many social, political, and economic trends in western Europe, metropolitan France, and the French colonies. This article includes numerous references to Martinique's delegates to the French Assembly and their arguments there as well as to events and economic conditions on the island. The second emancipation is put in its historical context, particularly in comparison with the British mode of abolition to which it aspired. The author modifies the usual portrayal of a peculiarly French, and hence revolutionary, approach to abolition that was supposedly characteristic of both the first and second republics.

131 **The campaign for the sugar islands, 1759.**
Marshall Smelser. Chapel Hill, North Carolina: The University of North Carolina Press, 1955. 212p.

This small volume is primarily about the battles waged in Martinique and Guadeloupe from January through to April of 1759 during the Seven Years War. It is a detailed, day-by-day account of the amphibious warfare engaged in by the British who, although they were repulsed from Martinique, captured and occupied Guadeloupe. The account is drawn from both British and French records but is written largely as a story of the British campaign to win the islands. There are valuable glimpses of the Martinican militia, the colonial inhabitants and their concerns, and the terms of the capitulation of Guadeloupe, which sent French officials and persons without property (privateers) to Martinique.

132 **Cannibal encounters. Europeans and island Caribs, 1492-1763.**
Philip P. Boucher. Baltimore, Maryland; London: The Johns Hopkins University Press, 1992. 217p. bibliog.

An important recent book, this examines the interaction between native Americans and Europeans in the Caribbean. It especially utilizes the French national archives for early sources and there are references to Martinique throughout. The author discusses the recent debate about the origins of island Caribs and their purported cannibalism. He traces the policies toward, actual treatment of, and images regarding the Caribs in both French and English colonies. Documents show a friendlier, more sympathetic French attitude toward and relationship with the Caribs than that practised by the British. He attributes the less hostile conditions between Amerindians and the French to the influence of French missionaries and the more active intervention and role of the French government. This volume is especially useful for its examination of persistent stereotypes regarding Caribs formed during the earliest period of contact.

133 **Case-Pilote, le Prêcheur, Basse Pointe. Étude démographique sur le nord de la Martinique. XVIIe siècle.** (Demographic study on the north of Martinique. 17th century.)
Liliane Chauleau. Paris: Éditions L'Harmattan, 1990. 188p. maps. illus.

The three locales which are the focus of this study were typical rural parishes of Martinique in the late 17th century. Primarily through the use of parish registers recorded by the Jesuits and Dominicans in 1680, 1700, and 1715, and augmented by contemporary regional histories, the author reconstructs parish social and demographic profiles. One chapter each is devoted to marriage data, birth rates, fecundity and fertility, and mortality. The demographic data – often displayed here in graphic and tabular form – reveal a great deal about life, customs, population structure, and religious practices during the first eighty years of French dominion on Martinique. The censuses of 1680 for Case-Pilote and le Prêcheur are printed in their entirety as supporting documents.

134 **Le Code Noir.** (The Black Code.)
William Renwick Raddell. *The Journal of Negro History*, vol. 10, no. 3 (July 1925), p. 321-29.

This short article concerns the substance of the contents of a 446-page volume published in 1770 on all French laws and regulations specifically related to the slave trade and the black slave. These were collectively known as the Code Noir and dated from 1685.

135 **Colbert's West India Policy.**
Stewart L. Mims. New Haven, Connecticut: Yale University Press, 1912. 335p. bibliog.

Based primarily on archival work in France, this is an original and scholarly study. It specifically develops the lines of policy toward the French West Indies of Jean-Baptiste Colbert, Minister of Finance to Louis XIV (1661-83). Colbert was the prime author of the mercantilist commercial policies that built up French industries and commerce in the 18th century; he established the West India Company to develop France's trade with Martinique and other colonies and to augment and control production of colonial commodities. There are chapters on colonial exports of tobacco and sugar and on imports, indentured servants and slaves, foodstuffs, and livestock, lumber, and manufactured items. Conditions on the islands are discussed primarily as they relate to and result from Colbert's policies. This volume is useful for an historical understanding of many economic and social patterns still existing in the Franco-Martinican relationship.

136 **Destinées d'esclaves à la Martinique.** (Slave conditions on Martinique.)
Gabriel Debien. *Bulletin de l'Institut Français d'Afrique Noire. Série B*, vol. 22, nos. 1-2 (1960), p. 1-91.

Reporting on slave life in Martinique, this lengthy document is based on lists and accounts in the French national archives covering the years 1746 to 1778. It examines the slave population by origin, age, and sex. A section each is devoted to agricultural work, domestics, trade work, households and families, Christian practices and names among the slave populations, demographic characteristics, fecundity, freedmen, and runaway and emancipated slaves. There are numerous age-sex pyramids for different years between 1746 and 1778. The article is indexed by place names, names of persons, and principal subjects.

137 **DuTertre and Labat on the 17th century slave life in the French Antilles.**
C. Jesse. *Caribbean Quarterly*, vol. 7, no. 3 (Dec. 1961), p. 137-57.

This article reports on the writings of DuTertre and Labat, two Dominican missionaries who lived in the French Antilles in the 17th century. Their copious writings have formed the basis of much knowledge about conditions during the first years after permanent European settlement on Martinique. The author systematically presents information on the introduction of slave labour into the Antilles, slave living conditions and provisions, and their character traits and comportment. Although Jesse writes sympathetically about early efforts to baptize and convert the slaves to Christianity, the two missionaries implied that most slaves continued to practise some sorcery.

138   **L'esclavage aux Antilles françaises. XVIIe-XIXe siècle.
Contribution au problème de l'esclavage.** (Slavery in the French
Antilles. 17th-19th century. Contribution to the problem of slavery.)
Antoine Gisler.   Paris: Éditions Karthala, 1981. 228p. bibliog.

In this volume, reprinted from the original 1965 edition, Gisler, a Dominican friar, has
examined a variety of primary and secondary sources to depict aspects of slavery in
the colonial French Antilles. The book's first section concerns the Code Noir, the edict
that officially regulated the treatment of slaves in the colonies; the daily life and work
conditions of slaves; and the comportment of their masters. The second part analyses
the institutional and juridical elements established to control and humanize the slave
trade, given that the entire society was caught up in slavery. The final section looks at
the church and missionaries and their relationship to slavery, namely: the role of clergy in reforms; petitions from parishes; the relationship to creole mentality; and the
lags between views embraced by the clergy and those of the civil administrators. The
author is particularly concerned with linking ethical and normative behaviour in
regard to slavery.

139   **L'esclavage aux Antilles françaises avant 1789.** (Slavery in the
French Antilles before 1789.)
Lucien Peytraud.   Paris: Librairie Hachette, 1897. 472p. bibliog.

Part one of this volume covers the French in the Antilles and the nature of the slave
trade. It includes early French settlement, concessions to French companies for enter-
ing the trade, African regions where slaves were sought, and the export and sale of
slaves in the American colonies. Part two treats the systems of slavery in the Antilles.
It covers the legislation affecting slaves and slavery; slave religion, morals, and
material condition; the civil rights of slaves; punishment; maroonage and revolts;
slaves taken to France; and the enfranchisement of slaves in the 18th century. This is a
fine account of slavery in Martinique and the other French Antillean colonies and is
based primarily on unedited documents from the French National Archives.

140   **French pioneers in the West Indies, 1624-1664.**
Nellis M. Crouse.   New York: Columbia University Press, 1940.
294p. bibliog.

Throughout the 17th century the French were the dominant colonial power in the
Lesser Antilles. This general narrative is concerned with the pioneer period; it shows
the connections between the early French settlements on St. Christopher, Guadeloupe
and Martinique and the commercial trading companies under whose charters the earliest settlements functioned. Although owner-governors and Dutch traders prospered,
there was chaos and discord from France's standpoint. This account ends in 1664
when the West India Company assumed responsibility for management and government in the Americas so that France would at last profit from its thriving West Indian
possessions. For this highly readable history the author relies heavily on contemporary
French observers, particularly DuTertre, but does not use footnotes. Crouse's critical
annotated bibliography of consulted works is also of use.

141 **The French slave trade in the eighteenth century, an old regime business.**
Robert Louis Stein. Madison: The University of Wisconsin Press, 1979. 250p.

This volume is based primarily on archival work in French port cities, particularly Nantes which was the main slaving port. The French slave trade has received far less attention from historians than the British trade, so this is a welcome general treatment. French slave traders, a conservative group of businessmen whose profits derived primarily from the sale of slaves, were influential in the old régime and were among its most active and prosperous merchants, dominating commercial policies in cities like Nantes. At the time of the French Revolution most had extensive property in both France and the West Indian colonies. There are some interesting references to the role of Martinique and Martinican businessmen in the colonial sale and dispersal of slaves in the early 18th century.

142 **The French West Indies in French policy on the eve of the American Revolution.**
Pierre H. Boulle. *Revista/Review Interamericana*, vol. 5, no. 4 (Winter 1975-76), p. 564-82.

Boulle examines the changes in French colonial policy caused by her defeat by England in the Seven Years War and by the terms of the Treaty of Paris in 1763. The changes included making the French West Indies the centre-piece of the much-reduced empire, a build up and professionalization of the navy, and a dramatic reform and revision of the French colonial compact (the *exclusif*). This new attention to planters' interests, and the well-being of the colonies in general, the author believes to be key to France's success in the War of American Independence. The article demonstrates the importance of Martinique to France's colonial policy in the 18th century.

143 **From chattel to person: Martinique, 1635-1848.**
Joan Brace. *Plantation Society in the Americas*, vol. 2, no. 1 (April 1983), p. 63-80.

This author pieces together a descriptive account of slaves' lives and of their fluctuating legal status in the period before emancipation. The article is based on the accounts of DuTertre and Labat, 16th- and early 17th-century chroniclers, the French Code Noir, and various other, Martinican codes. Problems arising around the granting of freedom, miscegenation, concubinage, and legitimacy are manifest in the great range of *de facto* and *de jure* conditions in pre-emancipation Martinique.

144 **La gaoulé: la révolte de la Martinique en 1717.** (Gaoule: the Martinican revolt of 1717.)
Jacques Petitjean-Roget. Fort-de-France: Société d'histoire de la Martinique, 1966. 579p.

The Martinican revolt against France in 1717 was triggered by government demands that island planters stop growing certain crops like cotton and cocoa, but most importantly that they cease trading with foreigners and henceforth do business only with French merchants. The revolt involved the island militia during an inspection by French authorities; many of the officers in charge of local militia were either planters or related to planters. This detailed account, drawn primarily from materials in the national archives, provides affiliations and interests of many on both sides of the action in Martinique, as well as a day-by-day account of the actual revolt and its aftermath.

145 **Les gens de couleur libres du Fort-Royal, 1679-1823. IX. Les grandes familles; X. Relations des libres avec les blancs; XI. Conclusion. Index des noms de personnes.** (Free people of colour in Fort-Royal, 1679-1823. IX. The major families; X. Relations of freedmen with whites; XI. Conclusion. Index of the names of individuals.)
E. Hayot. *Revue Française d'Histoire d'Outre Mer*, vol. 56, no. 203 (1969), p. 99-163.

This lengthy narrative is an account of the free blacks of Martinique from their earliest appearance in colonial accounts until their separateness from slaves was no longer rigidly maintained. Hayot shows how free blacks became tradesmen and occupied other vital economic roles in Martinique from the beginning of the 18th century. By the second half of the century they had prospered so as to become merchants and property owners, roles which kept them separate from slaves. The free blacks became organized hierarchically in a manner similar to the white population of France: the whitest in positions resembling the nobility; the richest in the role resembling moderate-size planters and merchants; and the blacks resembling *petit-blancs*. Genealogies of these families, who were tightly interwoven, are recorded from the public registries, with godparents and witnesses to marriages and births provided to demonstrate influence. Only in 1811 did free blacks break from their alliance with whites and consistently fight for emancipation.

146 **Guadeloupe, Martinique and commerce raiding: two colonies in conflict, 1797-98.**
H. J. K. Jenkins. *Revue Française d'Histoire d'Outre Mer*, vol. 78, no. 293 (1991), p. 465-75.

In 1794 the British began an eight-year occupation of Martinique while nearby Guadeloupe, after a brief occupation, was controlled by republican Victor Hugues. Hugues initially tried to extend his control to Martinique and other islands but, failing that, then engaged in intense privateering against the Martinican coastal trade and long-distance shipping. Both local patrol-vessels and British ships defended the island and its commercial interests. The hostilities between Guadeloupe and Martinique, though short-lived, had complex ramifications for British, French, and American interests both in the Caribbean and elsewhere.

147 **Historique des troubles survenus à la Martinique pendant la Révolution.** (History of the unrest in Martinique during the Revolution.)
Pierre-François-Régis Dessalles. Fort-de-France, Martinique: Société d'Histoire de la Martinique, 1982. 472p.

This account was written during the Revolution by a prominent citizen of Martinique. It reads as a chronological journal of the tumultuous period from 1788 to December

1790. Decrees, deliberations of the colonial assembly, letters, and court proceedings are an integral part of the text. All sides of the debate concerning loyalty to the king, the freeing of slaves, and economic issues are represented. This apparently lost manuscript was reprinted in a limited edition in 1982 and forms a vivid and thorough record of activities and sentiments on Martinique during the French Revolution.

148 **Marronage in the French Caribbean.**
Gabriel Debien. In: *Maroon societies: rebel communities in the Americas.* Edited by Richard Price. Garden City, New York: Doubleday Anchor, 1973. p. 107-34.
Debien looks at the underlying causes and basic characteristics of marronage in the colonial French Caribbean. Petit marronage, an absence of several days or a week, was the most common occurrence and was taken casually by managers and planters. Grand marronage, flight with no intention of returning, existed primarily among field and unskilled slaves. Collective marronage, however, sometimes in bands of up to several hundred individuals, was a serious crime and was vigorously pursued. This article, based on selections from the French National Archives, includes cases from Martinique and Guadeloupe and a review of punishments for all three types of marronage.

149 **Neither slave nor free: the freedmen of African descent in the slave societies of the New World.**
Edited by David W. Cohen, Jack P. Greene. Baltimore, Maryland: The Johns Hopkins University Press, 1972. 344p.
This collection of essays deals with the condition and roles of free people of colour in the Americas from the 16th to the 19th centuries. Chapter four, written by Léo Elisabeth (p. 134-171), is devoted to the French Antilles, Martinique and Guadeloupe, and to French Guiana. It covers legal codes applied to free persons of colour, manumission procedures, population and demography, marriage and childrearing, economic status, relations to the enslaved, resistance, and the effects of the French Revolution on the condition and attitudes of freed people in the colonies.

150 **La nourriture des esclaves sur les plantations des Antilles Françaises aux XVIIe et XVIIIe siècles.** (Slave nourishment on French Antillean plantations in the 17th and 18th centuries.)
Gabriel Debien. *Caribbean Studies*, vol. 4, no. 2 (1964), p. 3-27.
This article traces sources of nourishment and food for slaves in the 17th and 18th centuries. It reviews the rules and practices connected with planter-distributed provisions, the evolution of dooryard or kitchen gardens cultivated by slaves and the common food supplies which were generally composed of starchy root crops. Debien covers regional differences and the various combinations planters employed to try and solve the need to adequately feed their slaves. But on one thing all early chroniclers were strongly in accord and that is the fact that slaves were always undernourished and poorly fed. The travellers and colonists writing in the 18th century repeat these observations, recounting the great labour required by slaves to try and feed themselves when not working for planters. During drought and hurricanes great numbers of slaves perished from hunger and malnutrition.

151 **Les nouvelles Frances: France in America, 1500-1815, an imperial perspective.**
Philip P. Boucher.   Providence: John Carter Brown Library, 1989.
122p.

Some 133 primary sources were displayed at the John Carter Brown Library in 1989 for the bicentennial of the French Revolution and this volume was produced to accompany them. It is a well-written, beautifully illustrated history of the French enterprise in the Americas from the first French settlers until the Treaty of Vienna in 1815. The book (and collections) are important to note here because the Caribbean islands, including Martinique, occupy a central place in this interpretation. Although the stories of the French in Canada, the Mississippi Valley, and Haiti are more well-known, the islands of Martinique and Guadeloupe were always considered the most valuable possessions to France. Therefore this history, which puts the French Antilles in their rightful hemispheric perspective, is a good place for any student of Martinique to begin a study.

152 **One hundred million Frenchmen: the 'assimilation' theory in French colonial policy.**
Martin Leurs Deming.   *Comparative Studies in Society and History*, vol. 4 (1961-62), p. 129-53.

Examines the definition and application of assimilation (complete integration into the politics, economy, and cultural history of metropolitan France) as a French colonial policy. In the two Caribbean colonies of Martinique and Guadeloupe complete assimilation into French culture and politics was tied to the emancipation of slaves; former slaves, it was reasoned, had no other cultural tradition available to them than that of the metropolis. This article examines the built-in contradictions between assimilation theory and the undemocratic nature of colonialism and economic imperialism. It is invaluable for the light it sheds on why Martinique is now a French department, despite its colonial history and its location in the Caribbean.

153 **Une petite Guinée: provision ground and plantation in Martinique, 1830-48.**
Dale Tomich.   *Slavery & Abolition*, vol. 12, no.1 (1991), p. 68-91.

Tomich argues that slave subsistence gardening and commercial sugar production were bound together. Masters encouraged provisioning as a way of providing cheap labour but it also generated an autonomous life for slaves. This practice of giving slaves land and a free Saturday to grow their own food arrived in Martinique with the introduction of sugarcane plantations from Brazil. Despite the Code Noir of 1685, whereby the French government tried to establish uniform dietary standards for slaves in all colonies, slave provision grounds became increasingly important on Martinique. By the 1830s slaves were in fact supplying all local produce and had developed a thriving secondary market and economic network. With emancipation, the inevitable participation in production and marketing activities were encouraged as a transition to free labour status, and slave rights to gardens and their produce were acknowledged. The use of task work as an incentive to slaves became a widespread management tool. However, skills and resources allowed free blacks an alternative to plantation wage labour after emancipation and a bargaining position with planters.

154 **Les protestants à la Martinique sous l'ancien régime.** (Protestants in Martinique under the Ancient Regime.)
Jacques Petitjean-Roget. *Revue d'Histoire des Colonies*, vol. 40, no. 3 (1956), p. 220-65.

This article consists of a chronological accounting of records about Protestants and their rights, status, and activities on Martinique. The author draws his material from first-hand historical accounts and official documents in the colonial section of the national archives. Although Martinique, like other French colonies in the Americas, was initially banned to Protestants, Dutch Reformed and French Huguenots have been present there since the first days of the colony in 1635, particularly as merchants and sugar refiners. The article traces changing royal policies and their effects on Protestants in Martinique to 1787.

155 **Slavery in the circuit of sugar: Martinique and the world economy. 1830-48.**
Dale W. Tomich. Baltimore, Maryland: The Johns Hopkins University Press. 1990. 353p. bibliog.

This volume is a reconstruction of the historical development of slave labour and plantation agriculture in Martinique prior to emancipation in 1848. The author, in a well-documented study, attempts to unite the local history of plantation slavery on Martinique with the larger history of the capitalist world economy, using core-periphery relationships as his framework.

156 **The slaves and free colored of Martinique during the French Revolutionary Period; three moments of resistance.**
David Geggus. In: *The Lesser Antilles in the age of European expansion.* Edited by Robert Paquette, Stanley Engerman.
Gainesville, Florida: University Presses of Florida, 1993.

The author examines contemporary accounts of and common patterns in three incidences of unrest among slaves and free coloureds in Martinique between 1789 and 1811. He believes that it is most important to isolate and examine the appearance of a European anti-slavery movement in the late 1700s, which began earlier and lasted longer than the French Revolution and its political ideology. Slave resistance in colonies (including the three Martinican uprisings described here) is often tied to false rumours of emancipation decrees in the home country, and is especially reflected in the St. Pierre uprising of 1789. A second insurgency involved free coloureds and manumission during British military rule on Martinique in 1800. All three uprisings started in cities on Martinique, a rather uncommon characteristic of slave revolts.

157 **La société d'habitation à la Martinique. Un demi-siècle de formation. 1635-85.** (Settler society in Martinique. A half century of formation.1635-85.)
Jacques Petitjean-Roget. Paris: Librairie Honore Champion, 1980.
2 vols. 1,606p. bibliog.

Providing a comprehensive look at the earliest years of French settlement on Martinique, this major work is a doctoral dissertation submitted to the University of Paris. After chapters on the settling of the island, the nature of the colony, and the island environment and people, Petitjean-Roget divides the first fifty years into a four-part study. The first consists of the formative years from 1635-40 and tells of settlements, colonist make-up, early products and merchandise. A period of crises from 1640-50 involves the Jesuits, merchants, landowners, and governors and forms the second part. The third part, the years 1650-64, covers the eviction of native Americans, the diversity of the population, settlement, and the religious make-up of society. The final years, 1665-85, cover the young colony under royal administration and particularly the influence of Colbert. Petitjean-Roget proposes that by 1685 the elements of a polarized creole society were already solidly in place.

158 **Les troupes du roi à la Martinique, 1664-1762.** (The king's troops in Martinique, 1664-1762.)
Jacques Petitjean-Roget. *Revue Historique de l'Armée*, vol. 23, no. 3 (1967), p.16-33.
This article treats French troops on Martinique during the period of continuous French control between 1664 and 1762. Information comes primarily from documents in the colonial section of the French National Archives and treats such issues as the number of companies and soldiers stationed on the island, their pay, rations, weapons, desertions, and hardships. Although by the late 1600s some of the officers were from old creole families, the soldiers were generally young and undisciplined, and functioned largely as mercenaries on the margins of creole society. Never more than a few hundred men throughout the period studied, the French military existed in an almost feudal manner on the island.

159 **La vie d'un colon à la Martinique au XIXe siècle. Journal. 1842-47.** (The life of a planter in Martinique in the 19th century.)
Pierre Dessalles. Printed privately by Henri de Frémont, Léo Elisabeth, 1985. 4 vols.
This privately printed work consists of the correspondence and journal of Pierre Dessalles between 1808 and 1856. Dessalles was a member of a prominent landowning family as well as an advisor to the royal court in France. The journals contain much information on daily life and social relations in Martinique during the first half of the 19th century and include the period encompassing the emancipation of slaves.

160 **The West Indian slave laws of the eighteenth century.**
Elsa V. Goveia. *Revista de Ciencias Sociales,* vol. 4, no. 1 (1960), p. 75-105.
Spain, England and France were the three major European colonizing powers in the Caribbean and this paper is a useful comparative examination of their slave laws. It includes a lengthy section on the French Code Noir, which is valuable in showing how the Code Noir, although written in Europe, was promulgated expressly for the problems posed by West Indian slavery, and when it went against local custom – particularly on matters of concubinage and manumission of mulattoes – it was unsuccessful. The author concludes that, as they were actually administered in the 18th century, French slave laws differed much less from their English counterparts than previously thought. Actual practices point to an erosion of the early material provisions and legal benefits conferred on French slaves. The rule of force had similar results throughout the slave areas of the Caribbean, resulting from the need to maintain stability in the basic social organization that supported West Indian life.

161 **Why Sugar? Economic cycles and the changing staples on the English and French Antilles, 1624-54.**
Robert Carlyle Batíe. *The Journal of Caribbean History*, vol. 8-9 (1976), p. 1-41.
The first thirty years of European settlement in the Antilles were turbulent and while Barbados was quickly established as a sugar colony, the other island colonies continued to produce tobacco, cotton, indigo, and ginger. In contrast to the prevalent view that until sugar became widespread French and English colonies had only a marginal economic existence, the author maintains that there was great economic opportunity throughout the early period on all islands. He uses commodity price data, correspondence, and travel accounts to support his thesis. This is a useful, original, and well-documented treatment of economic cycles during the first years of the Antillean colonies, and it is all relevant to Martinique, to which there are numerous specific references.

162 **A Yankee trader views the French Revolution in Martinique.**
Thomas H. LeDuc. *The New England Quarterly*, vol. 11 (1938), p. 802-07.
This article is composed of a published letter written by Samuel R. Helms, a Rhode Island merchant stationed in St. Pierre, Martinique, in 1790. He writes colourfully of confrontations between French nationalists (union cockades) and citizens, which led the royalist governor to leave the island.

From emancipation to departmentalization (1848-1948)

163 **Louis des Étages (1873-1925). Itineraire d'un homme politique martiniquase.** (Louis des Étages [1973-1925]. Journey of a Martinican politician.)
Georges B. Mauvois. Paris: Éditions Karthala, 1990. 142p.
This monograph is an account of the political life and activities of Louis des Étages, who was elected to Martinique's General Council in 1907 and to the mayorship of Rivière-Salée in 1918. His life was contemporary with the mechanization and centralization of island distilleries and refineries and he was deeply involved in the earliest organization of workers. When Étages was assassinated in 1925 he had successfully participated in the establishment of a workers' movement and socialist presence in island politics.

164 **Le rôle des femmes dans l'insurrection du Sud de la Martinique en Septembre 1870.** (Womens' role in the September 1870 insurrection in southern Martinique.)
Odile Krakovitch. *Nouvelles Questions Feministes*, vol. 910 (Sept. 1985), p. 35-51.

The role of black Martinican women in the brief uprising of September 1870 is examined in this article. The uprising was centred in the Riviére-Pilote sector and comprised the most serious insurrection after the 1848 abolition of slavery. Twenty-five houses were burned and three people killed in an uprising that seemed to be spontaneous and without ideology. Fourteen women were condemned for incendiary activities and pillage; their sentences included one death and varying lengths of prison terms and forced labour in Cayenne. The article analyses how judges and witnesses, in trial accounts, attributed female participation to feminine instincts like curiosity and the spreading of fear through crimes like fire, poison, and theft. These crimes are traditionally associated with both blacks and women. The author discusses how these black women, the proletarians of the proletariat in late 19th-century Martinique, incurred the sentences commuted on them by the military court.

165 **Tamil emigration to Martinique.**
Xavier S. Thani Nayagam. *Journal of Tamil Studies*, vol. 1, no. 2 (Oct. 1969), p. 75-123.

From contemporary documents and publications, Nayagam describes conditions under which contract labourers were brought from India to Martinique between 1851 and 1883. Of the 25,500 who came, 15,000 died and nearly 12,000 repatriated; thus, even with more than 5,000 births on Martinique, the numbers of Indians on the island have never been high. Current Martinican surnames and other local records indicate that the vast majority of Indians were Tamil-speaking Hindus who came from Pondicherry and Karical. The author appraises the degree of acculturation and describes the loss of the Tamil language, religious rites, and folk customs. Appendices provide a list of 600 Tamil names from 19th century records and the place of birth for many of them.

166 **La vie quotidienne aux Antilles françaises au temps de Victor Schoelcher. XIX siècle.** (Daily life in the French Antilles in Victor Schoelcher's time. 19th century.)
Liliane Chauleau. Paris: Hachette littérature, 1979. 379p.

This book is a well-written, readable synthesis on 19th-century Martinique and Guadeloupe based on archival material and a wide range of secondary sources and travellers' accounts. Chauleau writes of the island setting, urban life, houses and gardens, education, culture, economy, and politics. Her portrayal is one of a quaint insular population more and more sensitized to political fights and economic problems in the years following Emancipation. Although the late 19th century was a time of political and economic change, Chauleau describes how the fabric of much of traditional Martinican life remained the same.

Recent history (1948 to present)

167 **The Caribbean: British, Dutch, French, United States.**
Edited by Curtis A. Wilgus.   Gainesville, Florida: University of
Florida Press, 1958. 331p.

Comprised of the proceedings of a 1957 conference that focused on the Caribbean by
political and geographical subgroups. Three papers treat the French areas, which
include Martinique, and cover political development, economy, and society. The
papers are all rather general summaries, with analyses reflecting an establishment-
oriented US foreign policy planning and development perspective.

168 **Europe in the Caribbean.**
Harold Mitchell.   Stanford, California: Stanford University, Hispanic
American Society, 1963. 211p. bibliog.

This volume provides an analysis of the policies of the Netherlands, Great Britain, and
France in the Caribbean. There is a short historical section, introductory to the bulk of
the book, which is devoted to post-Second World War events. One chapter treats post-
war French political aims and another, French economic policy. The author gives a
good accounting of the mood and situation on Martinique in the 1950s and early
1960s. He has drawn heavily from newspapers, including *Le Monde*, *Le Figaro*, and
the Martinican daily *Le Courrier*, which makes this a particularly valuable synthesis
and chronological account of recent history.

169 **The French Antilles and their status as overseas departments.**
Guy Lasserre, Albert Mabiteau.   In: *Patterns of foreign influence in
the Caribbean*.   Edited by Emanuel de Kadt.   London: Oxford
University Press for the Royal Institute of International Affairs, 1972.
p. 82-102.

The authors identify overpopulation, specialization in agricultural products, and
underemployment as special problems faced by the French Antilles, despite their
status as French departments. They conclude that political conversion into French
departments has not been successful: it eroded the political basis of power and has
been inadequate to deal with characteristic island underdevelopment. The authors
blame the political malaise affecting the island on the contact and clash between a
consumer French society and an underdeveloped Antillean society. Despite variations
in French policy, the authors believe that Martinican élites with vested interests in the
status quo are what primarily hinder either development or true regional autonomy.

170 **Metropolitan influences in the Caribbean: the French Antilles.**
Michael Horowitz.   *Annals of the New York Academy of Sciences*,
vol. 83 (1960), p. 802-08.

This paper is a brief but cogent presentation of Martinican history and in particular the
island's economic and political relationship to France. The article also outlines social
structure, employment, and political orientation. Although written in 1960, most of
Horowitz's observations remain relevant.

171 **La transformation des îsles d'Amérique en départements français.**
(Tranformation of the American islands into French departments.)
Victor Sablé.　Paris: Larose, 1955. 200p.

The author presents a chronological accounting of French royal edicts, ministerial policies, decrees, and other laws that have affected the status, rights, and obligations of
Martinique and its inhabitants. Sablé sees departmentalization in 1948 as a logical
political and economic outgrowth of 300 years of shared French and Martinican history. Sablé was a Martinican deputy to the French National Assembly at the time.

Population

General

172 **Les facteurs de la fécondité en Martinique.** (Fecundity factors in Martinique.)
Henri Léridon. *Population*, vol. 26, no. 2 (1971), p. 277-300.
This study is one of many which attempt to understand fecundity patterns on Martinique. It was prompted by the island's exceedingly high growth rate in the years after the Second World War and its already high population densities. Data for the study were gathered in 1968 and examine fecundity according to the following factors: type of marital union; number of marital unions and total time in union; level of literacy and education; socio-professional level; and place of residence. Only the last three variables show any correlation, and therefore possible explanatory roles, with fecundity variation.

173 **Fertility in Martinique.**
Henri Léridon. *Natural History*, vol. 79, no. 1 (Jan. 1970), p. 57-59.
A study of 1,600 Martinican women was begun in 1968 to look at fertility patterns according to three age groups and four categories of matrimonial status. The study, which is briefly summarized here, is an attempt to understand marital and childbearing patterns in the particular Martinican social milieu. Léridon mentions that contraception and birth control had only recently been introduced on the island but that the desire for conception was widespread. The study was prompted by the extremely high island population growth rate during the 1960s.

174 **Patterns of marital unions and fertility in Guadeloupe and Martinique.**
H. Léridon, Y. Charbit. *Population Studies*, vol. 35, no. 2 (1981), p. 235-45.

A study was made among 2,849 women between the ages of fifteen and forty-nine to shed light on the rapid fall in fertility on Guadeloupe (twenty-five per cent) and Martinique (forty per cent) in the ten-year period from 1965 to 1975. The authors here try to relate the decline to economic, social, and cultural factors, particularly union patterns (visiting, common law, and married). Data analysis is presented for fertility rates by type of union, for age- and union-specific fertility rates, and for fertility rates by complete union history. By utilizing all three types of analysis, the authors attempt a complex methodology that will account for varying individual union histories.

175 **Population policies and Caribbean crisis.**
Aaron Lee Segal. In: *Population policies in the Caribbean.* Edited by Aaron Lee Segal. Lexington, Massachusetts: D. C. Heath & Company, 1975. p. 1-25, 219-29.

Segal sees the demographic and social crisis of Caribbean societies in the early 1970s as a product of their political and economic situations. High birth rates, low infant mortality, long life spans, and high net emigration coupled with awareness of high living standards in North America and Europe have created this crisis. The situation in Martinique and the effect of French policies on island demographic statistics are considered; Segal then reviews six broad ideas that have characterized 20th-century Caribbean thinking about population, as well as the commitment of governments to family planning programmes.

Ethnicity

176 **Ethnological aspects of the Martinique creole.**
Vincent W. Byas. *The Journal of Negro History*, vol. 28, no. 3 (July 1943), p. 261-83.

A dated and romanticized survey of the historical literature, this attempts to account for patterns of miscegenation and the physical attributes of the black Martinican creole or mulatto. The author invokes the rationale behind such formal theories as hybrid vigour, environmental determinism, insularity, and allopatric speciation in trying to give validity to his undisguised admiration for the Martinican phenotype, which he believes to be an emergent 'race'.

177 **L'étude de la structure génétique d'une population métissé.** (Study of the genetic structure of a mulatto population.)
Jean Benoist. *Anthropologica*, vol. 3, no. 1 (1961), p. 55-64.

Benoist uses two studies of the mulatto population of Martinique, one by geneticists Montestruc and Berdonneau and the other, his own descriptive work with 232 Martinican men. The genetic study shows the association of independent characters but it alone cannot account for them. The combination of classical anthropological description of phenotypes and sexual patterns with the genetic work allows Benoist to state that the Martinican population still has a high genetic instability and low integration of its constituent racial groups. This type of racially-oriented physical anthropology is no longer widely engaged in by American scholars.

178   **Indians in the French overseas departments: Guadeloupe, Martinique, Réunion.**
Singaravélou.   In: *South Asian overseas, migration and ethnicity.*
Edited by Colin Clarke, Ceri Peach, Steven Vertovec.   Cambridge, England: Cambridge University Press, 1990. p. 75-87.

This chapter looks at demographic growth and distribution of the Indian population in the island departments of Guadeloupe, Martinique, and Réunion since 1946. The author then writes on socio-economic integration of the Indians, their religious and linguistic evolution, and the French policy of assimilation. In Martinique the Indian population is small, comprising no more than three per cent of the total population, is concentrated in the rural northern communes, and except for a few remnant traces of the Hindu religion, has lost virtually all signs of cultural distinctiveness.

Settlement

179   **Une cité planifiée et une cité spontanée. (Fort-de-France, Martinique.)** (A planned city and a spontaneous city. [Fort-de France, Martinique.])
Romain Paquette.   *Cahiers de Géographie de Québec*, vol. 13 (1969), p. 169-86.

Since the early 1950s the population of Fort-de-France, Martinique's capital, has expanded rapidly up the hillsides leading away from the old city and the harbour. This article examines the conditions of growth and population characteristics for two quite different districts during the period 1952 to 1968. La Trénelle is a spontaneous settlement – once a shantytown – and is over-whelmingly composed of residents born in the countryside; its progress derives from the initiatives and efforts of the people themselves. L'Ensemble Floreal, adjacent to La Trénelle, is a planned and heavily subsidized community with funds and expertise coming from France itself. It more closely resembles a true suburb, with higher proportions of white-collar workers and residents who are natives of Fort-de-France and have moved out from previous residences (and up in status).

180   **Urbanization and urban growth in the Caribbean.**
Malcolm Cross.   Cambridge, England: Cambridge University Press, 1979. 174p. bibliog.

This book-length essay is valuable because it discusses urbanization and the nature of urban growth for the entire Caribbean region, integrating literature from all historical and political divisions. Cross examines urbanization around theories on imperialism and core/periphery dependency, showing how dualism develops at three levels: between the former colony and the metropolis; between the country's primate city and its rural areas; and between unequal sectors of the primate city itself. The growth and dominance of the city are a response to consumption, with education and social organizations reinforcing colonial patterns. Although Martinique is specifically referred to a number of times, virtually all of the volume can be applied to Martinique's case. This essay provides a regional framework from which to study internal migration, rural and urban economies, and social change.

181 **Un village du bout du monde.** (A village at the end of the world.) Joseph Josy Levy. Montréal, Québec: Les presses de l'université de Montréal, 1976. 136p. maps.

Based on field work in Grand Rivière, Martinique, in 1968, this volume is an anthropological study of village structures and modernization there. It is a monographic treatment of the commune and village over the last 100 years, with many useful maps, graphs, and tables on land use, economic activity, and population structure. Individual chapters examine village history, the Bellevue plantation, fishing, gardening and animal keeping, and community and family structure. The author attempts to show how political changes, particularly departmentalization in 1948, have realigned village economic, sociopolitical, and demographic units.

Migration

182 **Afro-Caribbean migrants in France: employment, state policy, and the migration process.**
Stephanie A. Condon, Philip E. Ogden. *Transactions, Institute of British Geographers*, new series, vol. 16, no. 4 (1991), p. 440-57.

This paper is concerned with the role that Afro-Caribbean labour played in post-war French economic growth. It studies the occupational structure of Afro-Caribbean labour in France in 1982 and the French government's role in influencing that structure, particularly through migration policies. In a sample of 200 male and female migrants from Martinique and Guadeloupe, the authors demonstrate how migrants were directed to low level service jobs, were concentrated in the Paris region, and experienced high job instability and barriers to promotion. The key role of migrants from Martinique and Guadeloupe has been as a replacement labour force in the public sector. Nonetheless, migrants from the Caribbean departments fare better in France than their foreign migrant counterparts.

183 **Caribbean migration to Britain and France.**
Gary P. Freeman. *Caribbean Review,* vol. 11, no. 1 (Winter 1982), p. 30-33, 61-64.

The half of this article devoted to French immigration policies shows how post-Second World War France, with declining fertility rates and suffering from heavy war losses at home, actively encouraged the immigration of unskilled labourers from overseas colonies. It discusses the built-in contradictions between the overall French policy, as it became increasingly restrictive after 1972, and specific policies toward overseas departments such as Martinique. Because of the privileges of full French citizenship and rights during the 1970s, as many as one-third of all Martinicans were residing and working in France. The situation became even more complex when the Mitterrand government's stance favouring island self-determination was counterbalanced with the special political status and overall social protection that Martinicans already possessed.

184 **Emigration from the French Caribbean: the origins of an organized migration.**
Stephanie A. Condon, Philip E. Ogden. *International Journal of Urban and Regional Research*, vol. 15, no. 4 (1991), p. 505-23.

Postwar emigration from Martinique and Guadeloupe to mainland France is examined in this scholarly article. During the 1940s and 1950s migrants were recruited directly into domestic, military, and public sector work. The French government then became closely involved in recruitment and immigration, due to a strong labour demand in France and fears over political and demographic instability in the Caribbean islands. In 1962, demographically balanced migration quotas for the overseas departments were devised by the newly-organized Bureau of Migration. Migrant records for 1962-63 and 1967 show that a policy bias toward males in the early years became more sexually balanced by 1967. The authors argue that despite official statements there was widespread exploitation of cheap Caribbean labour and that training, housing, and general welfare from government sources were often no more than a façade.

185 **Le jeune antillais face à la migration.** (The young Antillean faced with migration.)
Pierre-Laval Sainte-Rose. Paris: Editions Caribéennes, 1983. 159p.

A questionnaire regarding emigration to France was administered to 138 Martinican students aged eleven to seventeen and this small volume presents the results. Because most emigrants are between the ages of sixteen and twenty-five, these young people are studied as potential migrants. A variety of questions on attitudes about and reasons for travel to France are administered and analysed as push-pull factors affecting migration. The overwhelming majority (eighty per cent) expect to migrate to France, with study, work, and learning a trade being the three principal reasons for going.

186 **Migration, natality, and fertility: some Caribbean evidence.**
Jerome McElroy. *International Migration Review*, vol. 24, no. 4 (1990), p. 783-802.

The author compares the relationship between the mobility of young women and fertility in ten heterogenous Caribbean sending countries, including Martinique, and two receiving countries. From government immigration and census records he constructs emigrant and immigrant profiles for the period 1960 to 1970. In Martinique and other labour-exporting countries, there is a pronounced natality and fertility decline.

Society and Social Conditions

General

187 **Anthropologie à la Martinique.** (Martinican anthropology.)
Francis Affergan.   Paris: Presses de la fondation nationale des
sciences politiques, 1983. 265p. bibliog.
This essay is a consideration of visible expressions of Martinican society – language,
names and words – and of social and psychological manifestations. The author
explores the many components and contradictions in Martinican space and identity,
drawing from a wide variety of publications in the social and behavioural sciences and
from the fine arts, to present a psycho-social portrait of the island.

188 **L'archipel inachevé.** (The unfinished archipelago.)
Edited by Jean Benoist.   Montréal: Les presses de l'université de
Montréal, 1972. 354p. bibliog.
This collection of papers is divided into four sections: socio-economic modes of adap-
tation and ecology; social organization; aspects of worldview; and social change. The
editor has written an introductory chapter on anthropological study in the Antilles and
a general conclusion and assessment. Five of the sixteen chapters are specifically
Martinican studies, but the entire collection will be of interest to the student of
Martinican culture and society.

189 **The birth of African-American culture.**
Sidney W. Mintz, Richard Price.   Boston: Beacon Press. 1992. 121p.
bibliog.
Originally published in 1976, this is an important and provocative book by two emi-
nent anthropologists. In it the authors present approaches for examining the
African-American past, discussing how African settlements and societies in the New
World differed from those of Europeans. They maintain that African-American
social and cultural forms were shaped through both the oppression of slavery and the

59

interdependence between slave and free sectors of society, thus giving rise to a distinctive new culture in the Americas.

190   **The Caribbean as a socio-cultural area.**
       Sidney W. Mintz.   In: *Peoples and cultures of the Caribbean.*
       Edited by Michael M. Horowitz.   Garden City, New York: The
       Natural History Press, 1971. p. 17-46.

Mintz argues that the societies of the Caribbean are in some ways the most 'Western' of all countries outside Western Europe and the United States. In this analysis he discusses nine characteristic features that he believes have given shape and expression to the regional commonality of Caribbean societies. This is a useful framework, which is wholly applicable to Martinique, by an eminent student of the Caribbean.

191   **Caribbean race relations. A study of two variants.**
       H. Hoetink, translated from the Dutch by Eva M. Horykaas.   London;
       Oxford; New York: Oxford University Press, 1971. 207p.

The author, a sociologist, specializes in pluralistic societies, whose distinct historical and cultural traditions he uses to explain variations in race relations in two types of Caribbean societies. The first is Iberian, with its unifying and universalizing Catholic tradition; the second is Northwest European, with its more commercial, individualistic orientation. Hoetink believes that French societies, although Catholic, align more closely with those of Northwest Europe. He cites the importance of the creole language, the existence of a small but distinct group of 'poor' whites, and strong intragroup endogamy as characteristics to confirm this placement. This entire volume provides a sociological framework through which Martinican society can be studied. There are several points at which Martinique's socio-economic and racial divisions are specifically discussed.

192   **Caribbean transformations.**
       Sidney W. Mintz.   Chicago: Aldine Publishing Company, 1974. 355p.
       bibliog.

This is a seminal work in Caribbean studies, an insightful scholarly treatment of the evolution of what Mintz terms 'Afro-Caribbeana'. By examining the everyday life of small island populations he shows both the unity and diversity in West Indian societies. The book is divided into three sections: slavery, forced labour, and the plantation system; Caribbean peasantries; and Caribbean nationhood. This volume may be used as the framework into which Martinique's history and society can be placed. Despite its date this is the best English-language social history of slavery and the plantation system, peasant agriculture, and market systems in the Caribbean and is based on case studies in Puerto Rico, Jamaica, and Haiti.

193   **Contacts de civilisations en Martinique et en Guadeloupe.**
       (Contacts between civilizations in Martinique and Guadeloupe.)
       Michel Leiris.   Paris: UNESCO/Gallimard, 1955. 192p.

A now-classic source of basic sociological information on Martinique and Guadeloupe this was researched between 1948 and 1952 as part of UNESCO's series on race and society. The first section examines the peopling of the islands, their social structure and regional life. In the second section Leiris discusses French culture in the islands, the role of schools, teachers, education, and culture in general and the problem of a specifically Antillean culture. The final section addresses racial prejudice, class, and relationships between white metropolitans from France and the diverse groups comprising native Antilleans. Leiris raises the following issues that still permeate daily life, politics, literature, and research in the French Antilles: overpopulation; migration; metropolitan government functionaries; and the *de facto* correlation between race, economic well-being, and status.

194 Identité Antillaise. (Antillean identity.)
Julie Lirus. Paris: Éditions Caribéenes, 1979. 266p. bibliog.

The author, a clinical psychologist and Martinican working in France, specializes in clinical applications of the Rorschach (ink blot) test. In this volume she reports and discusses her administration of the test to Martinican and Guadeloupean students in France in an attempt to determine their self image, social identity, and self representation. She observes that widespread inferiority complexes and negrophobia among Antillean students are the products of a history of slavery and assimilationism and are accompanied by anguish, fear, and exaggerated behaviour. From her study Lirus concludes that Antillean identity is distinct from Metropolitan or African self awareness and cultural identity.

195 Morne-Paysan. Peasant village in Martinique.
Michael M. Horowitz. New York: Holt, Rinehart, & Winston, 1967. 114p.

This monograph is a now-classic ethnographic decription of a highland peasant village of 1,650 persons that includes data on agriculture, households, conjugal relations, health, and religion. Morne-Paysan is characterized by extensive reciprocal kinship ties and obligations that unite its members into a community and obscure local class distinctions. The village is composed of small land owners, most of whom farm less than one hectare. Horowitz sees this way of life as doomed to disappear because of rapid population growth, the limited amount of land available, and the noncompetitiveness of locally produced food. Although varying socio-economic status is mentioned in the study, the emphasis is on the social advantages of kinship and mutual assistance. Conjugal relationships tend to be sequential among villagers, but landowners marry at far higher rates than wage labourers.

196 The so-called world system: local initiative and local response.
Sidney W. Mintz. *Dialectical Anthropology*, vol. 2, no. 4 (1977), p. 253-70.

Mintz attempts to substantiate the theoretical significance of Wallerstein's world economic system work by examining labour extraction from Caribbean plantations. This is a seminal paper for understanding plantation systems and society and the Caribbean region in their historical and economic contexts and is totally applicable to Martinique.

197 **Les sociétés antillaises. Études anthropologiques, 4éme édition.**
(Antillean societies. Anthropological studies, 4th edition.)
Edited by Jean Benoist. Montréal: Université de Montréal, Centre de
Recherches Caraïbes, 1975. 177p. bibliog.

This collection includes papers by a group of distinguished Caribbeanists on vital topics such as plantation culture, social types, markets and rural life, and the Caribbean
family. Two papers are on specifically Martinican topics: In 'Racial components in
Martinique', p. 13-29, Jean Benoist elaborates on the racial and ethnic groups represented on the island. Interracial mixing, always open, is resulting in an ever-more
homogeneous population, as biological types follow more fluid social relationships. In
'Precausal thought in a group of Martinican children', p. 105-43, Guy Dubreuil and
Cecile Boisclair apply Piaget's model on childhood thought development to seventy-
two Martinican students between four and twelve years old. They compare the results
to those from a sample of 400 Montreal students, examining five modes of precausal
thought – animism, realism, dynamism, finalism, and artificialism.

198 **A typology of rural community forms in the Caribbean.**
Michael M. Horowitz. *Anthropology Quarterly*, vol. 33, no. 4 (1960),
p. 177-87.

Horowitz presents a typology based on his own study of the Morne-Paysan commune
on Martinique and seven additional studies on other Caribbean islands and in British
Guiana, all conducted in the 1950s. He proposes that peasant life with agricultural
activity oriented to subsistence and some local sales, results in a tightly organized or
closed community with extensive kinship obligations, endogamy, ethnic homogeneity, and social equality. Where peasants emphasize cash crops and supplement
income with work in mines or sugar estates, communities are ethnically complex and
stratified. Open communities are associated with plantation wage labour; an agrarian
proletariat has the class distinctions, mixed ethnicity, limited kinship obligations, seasonal labour influxes, and greater anonymity more often associated with urban
industrial centres.

199 **West Indian societies.**
David Lowenthal. London; New York; Toronto: Oxford University
Press, 1972. 385p. bibliog.

This volume is a *tour de force* by an eminent American geographer. It is the essential
starting point for any social science work on the Caribbean or any of its islands.
Lowenthal incorporates an array of literature to provide a solid synthesis of the entire
region and simultaneously convey the great variation among component islands. The
volume covers social structure, race, cultural pluralism, migration, colonialism,
population, and identity. There are numerous specific references to Martinique and to
the writings of Martinicans.

Social structure and class

200 **Ambiguités des modèles et spécifité de la société martiniquaise.**
(The ambiguity of models and the specifics of Martinican society.)
François Gresle. *Revue Française de Sociologie*, vol. 12, no. 4
(Oct.-Dec. 1971), p. 528-49.

Gresle's sociological study attempts to explain the evolution of Martinique's complex society and how this complexity has contributed to an inability to articulate a strong and separate political identity. He argues that plantation society has been continued in the rigid social roles that characterize present-day Martinique. This polarized and stratified society has a dual religious and belief system, one that is official and outward, another that is 'primitive' and animistic. Sexual behaviour, too, has two value systems, also inherited from the plantation society. The author proposes that all the African and European components of the Martinican social and economic system, despite modifications in the plantation and insular environment, remain viable. The overwhelming duality that pervades island life, however, is only an illusionary choice and the population seems paralysed in ambiguity, without a sense of community or shared destiny. The economic sector is sharply divided between service sector functionaries and labourers in the private sector. In politics, élite white *Békés* have long been electing black politicians who have maintained their interests.

201 **Comparaison des relations interpersonnelles dans trois communautés martiniquaises.** (Comparison of interpersonal relations in three Martinican communities.)
Joseph Josy Levy. In: *L'archipel inachevé*. Edited by Jean Benoist.
Montréal: Les presses de l'université de Montréal, 1972. p. 133-48.

In a brief chapter Levy compares his own research on the village of Grand Rivière with that of Richard Price on Belle-Anse and of Michael Horowitz on Morne-Paysan. In the isolated village of Belle-Anse relations outside the nuclear family are rare and strained; in Grand Rivière economic units are largely familial but leisure activities between neighbours are common and serve to renew community bonds and reduce tension; in Morne-Paysan (Morne-Vert) reciprocal economic ties outside the family are permanent and serve to integrate large sectors of the community. Levy links these observations with the work of Pelto and MacGregor, suggesting that hostility decreases within peasant communities to the degree that they are integrated into urban industrial centres. He also allows for investigator bias in the overall portrait of each community.

202 **A dominant minority: the white creoles of Martinique.**
Edith Kovats-Beaudoux. In: *Slaves, freemen, citizens: West Indian perspectives*. Edited by Lambros Comitas, David Lowenthal.
Garden City, New York: Doubleday Anchor, 1973. p. 240-75.

This chapter is an analysis of the rigid social differentiation in Martinique. The author shows how high endogamy within four white subgroups, and between races, serves the economy and fixes Martinican social structure. Legal mixed marriages are uncommon and excessive social pressure to maintain racial purity guarantees the perpetuation of inequality. Kovats-Beaudoux indicates that recent closer relations with the metropolis are having some effect on this rigid, long-extant social structure. Martinique's small white minority (well less than five per cent of the island's total population) has been given disproportionate representation in academic studies and literature, of which this is one example.

203 Land tenure and class in Morne-Vert.
Willie L. Baber. *Anthropology*, vol. 8, no. 2 (1985), p. 41-54.
Baber, a self-defined Marxist, explains his own 1976 observations in Morne-Vert in relation to those of Horowitz, made in 1956. He argues that by the time of his study, wealth differentiation had become pronounced due to immigration to the village of wealthy Martinicans and a decline in the viability of a peasant way of life. Baber attempts to explain and contextualize these changes by means of a complex theoretical framework.

204 Political economy and the plantation system: a note on the Baber-Horowitz debate.
Willie L. Baber. *Anthropology*, vol. 10, no. 1 (1986), p. 33-42.
Baber attempts to establish his own study of Morne-Vert, Martinique, within an historical framework and in the context of larger regional processes by use of a political economic perspective. He continues to shadow box with Horowitz on the need to put all community-based studies into a larger systems context and to include a class analysis in them.

205 Political process in Morne-Vert: a note on the economizing strategy.
Willie L. Baber. *Anthropology*, vol. 8, no. 1 (1984), p. 1-11.
This paper applies Barth's social process model as an economizing strategy in political change in Morne-Vert, Martinique. Baber maintains that this strategy depends on community-level data, such as that gathered by Horowitz, that presupposes homogeneity and thus only partially describes social relations. Although this type of data can be useful, Baber maintains that without a theoretical conceptualization of history, such studies are inadequate and the models themselves become a tautology. Baber uses this discussion to criticize Horowitz.

206 Race and stratification in the Caribbean.
M. G. Smith. In: *Corporations and society*. London: Duckworth, 1974. p. 271-346.
The author, an anthropologist, analyses racial aspects of social stratification in West Indian societies. He believes that stratification is shown in the unequal distribution of resources, opportunities, rewards, and sanctions among members of a society. In Caribbean societies that are racially heterogeneous, such as Martinique, racial identity and differences are usually prominent among the measures of stratification. The paper discusses the historical development of racially distinct societal segments and presents racial structures. Smith points out general characteristics shared by most Caribbean creole societies as well as particular differences among them; Martinique's historical and contemporary situations are part of this comparative treatment.

207 **Social change and the peasant community: Horowitz's Morne-Paysan reinterpreted.**
Willie L. Baber. *Ethnology*, vol. 21, no. 3 (July 1982), p. 227-41.
In 1976 and 1977, nearly twenty years after Michael Horowitz (see *Morne-Paysan: peasant village in Martinique*), Baber carried out field work in Morne-Vert. In this self-proclaimed 'restudy', Baber contends that the village has changed, that it is no longer isolated, and that categorizing it as an egalitarian or peasant community is questionable. His macro-level description of the island economy includes statements on the impact of modernization on Morne-Paysan. For Baber to frame his own work in terms of Horowitz's community-level study is somewhat confusing and perhaps counterproductive to the value of each study.

208 **The unholy trinity.**
Anseleme Remy. *Caribbean Review*, vol. 6, no. 2 (1974), p. 14-18.
The author, an anthropologist at Fisk University, discusses how a Martinican's social position is established by wealth, degree of caucasoid features, and adherence to European culture. These three, Remy maintains, are the 'unholy trinity' that contribute to a rigid and divisive social structure or ethno-classes on Martinique. While ethnicity is an important characteristic of Caribbean society, he asserts, it is fossilized by Western bourgeois concepts. This keeps Caribbean peoples divided and prevents them from uniting against the colonial and neo-colonial systems that continue to oppress them.

209 **Urban poverty in the Caribbean. French Martinique as a social laboratory.**
Michel S. Laguerre. London: MacMillan, 1990. 181p. bibliog.
This original and scholarly book focuses on urban poverty in Fort-de-France, Martinique. The author proposes that poverty is a product of the island's plantation economy and dependence on metropolitan France. LaGuerre sees the reproduction of poverty through a continuous structure of inequality and power domination. Individual chapters consider the urban household, domestic workers, the grocery store, savings associations (*sousous*), and immigrant households as institutions and mechanisms that help explain and contribute to the creation and reproduction of poverty. Each of these factors functions to create assymmetrical relations between dominant and dominated sectors of society. While Laguerre believes the poor are struggling to escape their poverty, he attempts to show that the individual, culture, and state function in complementary ways to keep them from succeeding.

Family structure and gender

210 **The Caribbean family: legitimacy in Martinique.**
Miriam K. Slater. New York: St. Martin's Press, 1977. 264p. bibliog.
This is a seminal study on marriage and family structure based on community-level field work conducted on Martinique in 1956. Slater challenges the presumption of a standard, universal rule of legitimacy. Her work shows that no single conjugal

arrangement is looked upon as ideal in Martinique. Child production, child rearing, and marriage do not necessarily coincide to produce a universally desired type of family organization. There exists on the island a confusing history of religious, cultural, and economic values and practices which, Slater argues, have resulted in basic conflicts regarding marriage and legitimacy. This work shows how Western values on marriage and inheritance are not really applicable to Martinique. While this is a case study from Martinique, its findings apply to most of the plantation Caribbean.

211 **A decision model of conjugal patterns in Martinique.**
Michael M. Horowitz. In: *Peoples and cultures of the Caribbean.*
Edited by Michael M. Horowitz. Garden City, New York: Natural
History Press, 1971, p. 476-88.

Horowitz attempts to explain why particular conjugal relationships are chosen at specific ages by men, following a sequential pattern he observed in Martinique. He argues that the primary factor in heterosexual co-residence is the acquisition of land, and that having an established household then allows men sanctioned access to markets where women monopolize transactions of salable domestic garden produce.

212 **Documents on medical anthropology.**
By a French army surgeon, edited by Charles Carrington. Huntington,
New York: Robert E. Krieger, 1972. 2 vols.

Originally published in Paris in 1898, this unusual volume is what the author calls 'a psychological sketch of the history of the sexual passions of the human race', carried out in his capacity as a surgeon with the French army. He spent several weeks on Martinique en route to French Guiana, long enough to make some observations on race and morality. If nothing else, this is amusing reading during a long stint in a library and tells as much about Victorian tastes as it does about the physique and sexual habits of those written about.

213 **La famille martiniquaise: analyse et dynamique.** (The Martinican
family: analysis and dynamics.)
Guy Dubreuil. *Anthropologica*, vol. 7, no. 1 (1965), p. 103-29.

Presents a descriptive classification and analysis of Martinican families in a rural community. Patrifocal homes are oriented around nuclear families, legally recognized children, and economic independence. They tend to be closed, rigid units. Matrifocal homes, however, are characterized by elasticity, a state of constant change among members, economic collaboration, and ambivalence. In the 'ideal' Martinican society, the man seeks to preserve his land rights and paternal inheritance rights. In reality, poverty prevents many farmers from thinking long term. The conflicting value system of fathering many children to indicate masculinity and to receive immediate gratification means that most landless men and small landowners operate under matrifocal systems. Dubreuil proposes a model of these opposing value systems, whose operation serves to reinforce socio-economic inequalities of the patrifocal and matrifocal groups. This work complements that of Horowitz in 1967 (q.v.) and Slater in 1987 (q.v.).

214 **Famille et nuptialité dans la caraibe.** (Marriage and family in the Caribbean.)
Yves Charbit. Paris: Presses universitaires de France, Institut National d'Études-Démographiques, 1987. 413p. bibliog.

This volume is based on the author's extensive demographic research in Martinique, Guadeloupe, Jamaica, Guyana, and the Dominican Republic in the 1970s as part of the World Fertility Survey. Charbit believes that the heritage of slavery, migration, and plantation economy have had important effects on present-day marriage and family patterns, resulting in matrifocality and pluripaternity. A demographic analysis of marriage – which includes patterns of consensual unions, children from the first union, comparison of the first union and the actual matrimonial statute, the number of partners, and mean duration of unions – is presented for each of the countries listed above. A final section looks at the family and nuptiality. This is a useful volume because it includes similarities and differences among the West Indian countries surveyed, including Martinique.

215 **A note on marriage in Martinique.**
Michael M. Horowitz, Sylvia H. Horowitz. *Marriage & Family Living*, vol. 25, no. 2 (1963), p. 160-61.

Alternative conjugal relationships in a Martinican peasant village are treated in this brief article. It discusses two types of legal marriage, coresidence without marriage (*menáge*), and three categories of a child's birth status which determine inheritance rights. While broadly similar to marriage patterns elsewhere in the Caribbean, the authors note some differences in Martinique.

216 **The rule of legitimacy and the Caribbean family: a case in Martinique.**
Miriam K. Slater. *Ethnic Groups*, vol. 1, no. 1 (1976), p. 37-87.

Slater conducted field work in a sugar plantation area of Martinique in 1958 in an attempt to shed light on Malinowski's universal rule of legitimacy. Based on her findings, Slater argues that non-élite groups in Martinique show a continuum of marital union types, which she believes may be transitional to establishing an ideal of legitimacy. Slater does not see marital union patterns on Martinique as being deviant from a previously accepted élite (European) norm, but believes they result from the particular social and economic history of the island.

217 **Union patterns and family structure in Guadeloupe and Martinique.**
Yves Charbit. *International Journal of the Sociology of the Family*, vol. 10, no. 1 (1980), p. 41-66.

This paper is based on data gathered in 1975-76 that compared the stability of 'visiting', common-law, and legal marital unions. The demographic characteristics of the three types of union are quite similar based on the study of household and family structures, family relationship data, and the roles of male and female partners.

Language

218 **Discreteness and the linguistic continuum in Martinique.**
Claire Lefebvre. *Anthropological Linguistics*, vol. 16, no. 2 (1974),
p. 47-78.

Martinican speech is analysed in this paper in the light of the two prevailing approaches
to linguistic variation: the first proposes that all members of a community share a
single grammar with linguistic variation; and the second proposes that linguistic
heterogeneity in a community derives from more than one basic grammar and is
expressed as gradations. Lefebvre's study is based on work in 1970 and 1971 with
informants in a Martinican community where French-based Creole coexists with
French. Lefebvre scales local speech varieties employing several linguistic variables
and shows that speakers' own perceptions of that diversity correspond to the socio-
linguistic model. She argues that all speech patterns on Martinique fall within a two-
code system and conform to the second approach above. She found a consistency in
the use of Creole subsystems and that variance in French corresponded to differing
competence. All informants speak the mother-tongue of Creole well, but 'a standard
variety' of French is viewed in normative terms.

219 **Langage et folklore martiniquaise.** (Language and Martinican
folklore.)
Stany Delmond. *Mercure de France*, vol. 264, no. 898 (1935),
p. 83-85.

The author, who grew up in Martinique, writes descriptively on the island's creole
language, noting the derivation of many words and the simplification in grammar from
French. There are brief sections of creole proverbs, enigmas, children's songs, folklore on the subject of rum and popular music. The article treats creole speech and
folklore in a charming sort of way and not at all systematically or analytically.

220 **A linguistic perspective on the Caribbean.**
Mervyn C. Alleyne. In: *Caribbean contours.* Edited by Sidney W.
Mintz, Sally Price. Baltimore, Maryland; London: The Johns
Hopkins University Press, 1985. p. 155-79.

This article reviews the development of creole languages, the correlation of creole
with social class, and current views regarding the genesis of Caribbean creoles.
Diglossia, the term applied to the linguistic situation in Martinique, is placed in context. It involves the existence of two codes that share the same basic vocabulary but
differ in grammar and pronunciation; moreover, the two are used in mutually exclu-
sive domains. Alleyne writes about the current cultural and political climate in
Martinique where, as of 1985, the French government had approved the use of creole
in the elementary school system.

221 **The origin of West Indian creole languages: evidence from
grammatical categories.**
Douglas Taylor. *American Anthropologist*, vol. 65, no. 4 (1963),
p. 800-14.

The author is an authority on Caribbean creole languages and here he examines
Martinican, a Haitian creole, and Sranan, the English-vocabulary creole of Suriname.
He posits from the grammatical evidence that all three languages have incorporated a
formal category, aspect, mood, and tense not found in French and English. He believes
Africans brought to the West Indies as slaves were already familiar with an Afro-
Portuguese pidgin and that it forms the framework on which pidgins and creoles have
been built through lexical replacement.

222 **Le verbe en créole martiniquais.** (The verb in Martinican creole.)
Elodie Jourdain. *West-Indische Gids*, vol. 35, no. 1-2 (1954),
p. 39-58.

Jourdain presents a description of verbs and their usage in Martinican creole. After a
short section on the origin of creole verb types, there is a long treatment of impersonal
and ordinary verbs, transitive and intransitive verbs, active and passive verbs, and pro-
nomial and auxillary verbs as they are expressed in creole. Examples of verb forms –
persons, conjugation, modes, and voices – constitute the article's final section. Many
French grammatical forms do not exist in creole. This readable account focuses on
usage, examples, and description in creole construction. It contains almost no theoretical or linguistic tracings and analysis but is a good introduction to Martinican creole.

Religion

223 **Les Adventistes du Septième Jour aux Antilles françaises: anthropologie d'une espérance.** (Seventh Day Adventists in the French Antilles: anthropology of hope.) Raymond Massé. *The Canadian Review of Sociology and Anthropology*, vol. 15, no. 4 (1978), p. 452-65.

The Seventh Day Adventist Church and sects such as the Jehovah's Witnesses began to grow rapidly in the French Antilles in the 1960s. The author ties the success of these religious groups to rapid post-war social changes affecting Martinique and Guadeloupe. Adventism, with its emphasis on the Second Coming and premillenial tribulations, has offered solace and hope to lower class members during the often overwhelming economic and socio-political developments of recent years. It has also functioned as an alternative to nationalist and leftist political ideologies and allowed members to hold conservative political positions. The article is divided into sections focusing on a comparison of Adventists with the general Martinican population, the psychological aspect of conversion, how Adventism relates to popular religion, the relationship between socio-economic change and religious change, and Adventist ideology as an attitude of social and political abdication.

224 **Avatars du vodou en Martinique.** (Avatars of vodun in Martinique.) Gerson Alexis. *Conjonction*, vol. 126 (June 1975), p. 33-48.

Compares the religious climate and practices of Martinique with those of Haiti. Alexis observes that Martinique is an overwhelmingly secular society and islanders display almost an indifference to religious matters, making his study difficult. Catholic rituals like baptism he sees as having more social than religious significance. Because of the two societies' vastly different socio-political histories, animistic cults on Martinique are relegated to a reluctantly acknowledged subculture strongly influenced by East Indians rituals, whereas on Haiti vodun is a dynamic, openly practiced part of daily life.

225   **Les indiens de Guadeloupe et de Martinique.** (The Indians of
      Guadeloupe and Martinique.)
      Laurent Farrugia.   Paris: A. P. Collet, 1975. 179p.
This volume examines cultural manifestations of Hindu origin on Martinique and
Guadeloupe. It includes descriptions of ceremonies, dances, prayers, chants, stories,
myths, temples, and idols associated with East Indians in the islands. The author tries
to explain the symbolism involved and the syncretic contributions of Christianity and
Hinduism. There are many photographs to illustrate rituals and shrines.

226   **The Martiniquan East Indian cult of Maldevidan.**
      Michael M. Horowitz, Morton Klass.   *Social and Economic Studies*,
      vol. 10, no. 1 (1961). p. 93-100.
East Indians on Martinique are among the poorest people on the island. This article
briefly describes ritualistic activities of the syncretic cult of Maldevidan, which the
authors believe functions to provide socio-cultural support to lower class East Indians.
Practices resemble those of Hindu village India, but are interpreted with Roman
Catholic theology; deities are identified with Catholic saints; and ritualistic sacrifice
and feasting are connected with health, mate selection, and economic activities.

227   **Martinique, the isle of those who return.**
      Cecilia M. Egan.   *Natural History*, vol. 52, no. 2 (1943). p. 52-3, 96.
This article is a short description of religious ritual dances and plant and animal sacrifice at St. Pierre in 1939. The author acknowledges the loose fusion or syncretism
among religions on the island. The ritual she describes has definite Hindu and African
elements, of which drumming and blade walking are the most distinctive.

228   **Vodou et quimbois: essai sur les avatars du vodou à la Martinique.**
      (Vodun and quimbois: essay on the avatars of vodun in Martinique.)
      Gerson Alexis.   Port au Prince: Les Éditions Jardin. 71p.
The author, a Haitian journalist, considers local expressions of vodun, quimbois, and
Hindu rituals on Martinique in the context of the island's political and social situation.
He discusses the differences between vodun as practiced in Martinique and Haiti in
light of the two countries' vastly different political and cultural histories.

229   **The worship of South Indian deities in Martinique.**
      Michael M. Horowitz.   *Ethnology*, vol. 2, no. 3 (1963), p. 339-46.
The small, but visible East Indian population of Martinique perpetuates Hindu reli-
gious ceremonies despite the disapproval of the Roman Catholic Church, to which the
Indians also belong. This paper connects the ritualistic Hindu practices to their East
Indian counterparts and discusses them in terms of ritual prophylaxis and purification.
Horowitz, who studied on Martinique in the late 1950s, sees this syncretic local cult as
a means of reinforcing community and individual networks and of preserving cultural
identity among East Indian Martinicans.

Politics and Administration

Politics

230 **Les Antilles sans complexes.** (Antilles without complexes.)
Victor Sablé.   Paris: G.-P. Maisonneuve & Larose, 1972. 309p.

This is an interesting volume in which Victor Sablé, Martinican deputy to the Senate and French National Assembly, has published a collection of political positions and mandates he exercised from 1946 until 1972. His conservative assimilationist views contrast strongly with those favouring autonomy or separation from France.

231 **Assimilation or independence? Prospects for Martinique.**
Richard D. E. Burton.   Montreal: McGill University, Centre for Developing Area Studies, Occasional Monograph Series, no. 13, 1978. 69p.

The historical alternation between authoritarian and republican governments both in France and Martinique the author believes is critical to the development of the political paradoxes that characterize the island. Republican French régimes promoted assimilation, thereby depreciating island uniqueness; empires and the Vichy régime, on the other hand, have supported the hegemony of local white *Békés* and an island-based system. Non-white Martinicans voted overwhelmingly in favour of departmentalization in 1946, but creole political leaders were outspoken about its failure in the 1970s and their new desire for autonomy from France. The monograph also examines the economic disequilibrium, emergent capitalist class structure, endangered creole culture, and political expression characteristic of the departmental period. The author concludes that there is no middle ground between unsuccessful departmental status and independence and that the many Martinican political factions need to unite and convince islanders of the need to go their separate way from France.

232 **Black Frenchmen: the political integration of the French Antilles.**
Arvin Murch. Cambridge, Massachusetts: Schenkman Publishing,
1971. 156p. bibliog.

This study is based on the author's hypothesis that the French Antilles chose assimilation to metropolitan France because island political leaders have been relatively
satisfied with social conditions and were thus willing to work for greater equality in
association with France. He uses surveys and statistics to compare the British and
French Caribbean in terms of equality, social characteristics, and the political attitudes
of the top leaders. Murch also explores the belief that political independence may not
be feasible in the French Antilles and what he perceives to be an unusually strong
acceptance among Martinican leaders of metropolitan romanticism and culture.
Murch's study may be seen as sympathetic to the status quo because it does not look
beyond the hypothetical to actual conditions and awareness among the population at
large. The results of this study in attitudes among the political élite have been widely
cited in subsequent literature on Martinique's paradoxical political situation.

233 **Césaire et le Parti Progressiste Martiniquais: progressive
nationalism.** (Césaire and the Martinican Progressive Party:
progressive nationalism.)
Armet Auguste. *Nouvelle Optique*, vol. 1, no. 2 (1971), p. 57-84.

Auguste looks for contradictions and consistencies between Césaire's written political
thought and his political actions, from his resignation from the Communist Party in
1956 to his position in 1970 espousing autonomous self-rule for Martinique within the
French Assembly. The author accuses Césaire of being himself a victim of bourgeois
European culture; he sees Césaire's 'progressive' stance as a form of neo-assimila-
tionism, far from the writer's nationalistic affirmations of the 1950s.

234 **Elections and ethnicity in French Martinique: a paradox in
paradise.**
William F. S. Miles. New York: Praeger, 1986. 284p. bibliog.

In the 1981 French presidential election Martinique voted overwhelmingly for Giscard
d'Estaing while France was electing socialist François Mitterrand. This book is an
examination of why this was the case. Through an analysis of recent voting patterns,
Miles tries to explain why Martinique is among the few French colonies not to have
undergone decolonization. He concludes that Martinique's chronic political and social
issues of unemployment, migration, and nationalism were in limbo during the relative
prosperity following departmentalization in 1948. This and fear of the unknown he
connects with increasingly conservative voting in presidential elections. Martinican
voters, rather than displaying self-awareness, react to developments in the metropolis.
Miles concludes that, particularly after the new cultural programmes of the Mitterrand
government, the likelihood of an independent Martinique is remote and probably not
viable.

235 **Enemies of empire.**
John Gaffar LaGuerre. St. Augustine, Trinidad: University of the
West Indies, 1984. 262p. bibliog.

This is a study of the social and political thought held by French intellectuals on colonialism and neo-colonialism. Martinicans Aimé Césaire and Frantz Fanon are two of

73

the three individuals whose writings are examined and who the author believes are representative of trends within the French empire. This volume, which was originally a doctoral dissertation at the University of Manchester, is noteworthy because the author is a Trinidadian. He sees the issues to which Césaire and Fanon have responded as the beginnings of a search for black nationalism and more particularly, for a Caribbean destiny.

236 **France in the Caribbean.**
Helen Hintjens. In: *Europe and the Caribbean.* Edited by Paul Sutton. London: MacMillan, 1991. p. 37-69.

This chapter examines the cultural, social, economic, and political aspects of French presence in its three Caribbean-area departments. The author treats them as examples of centre-periphery relations involving varying degrees of conflict and collaboration between the overseas departments and France. She explores the search for a Caribbean identity, how migration to France is related to social policy (forty per cent of Martinicans now live in metropolitan France), ongoing economic transformations and dependence, and political life in the French Caribbean. In a final, separate section she reviews French foreign policy in the Caribbean region and compares France's de-colonization model and activities with those of Great Britain and the United States.

237 **Grenada, the Caribbean and the EEC.**
Scott B. MacDonald, Albert L. Gastmann. In: *The Caribbean after Grenada: revolution, conflict, and democracy.* Edited by Scott B. MacDonald, Harald M. Sandstrom, Paul B. Goodwin, Jr. New York: Praeger, 1988. p. 229-50.

A section is included in this chapter that specifically treats the impact of the US invasion in Grenada on French policy in the Caribbean. The authors see recent French policies in the region as stemming both from ideological considerations and from a determination of how area governments and economies might affect the stability of Martinique and the other overseas departments. There is a discussion of the prospects for a more progressive and vital role for the European Economic Community in the Caribbean. The chapter includes much material that specifically relates to Martinique.

238 **Guadeloupe-Martinique: a system of colonial domination in crisis.**
Philippe Alain Blérald. In: *Crisis in the Caribbean.* Edited by Fitzroy Ambursley, Robin Cohen. New York: Monthly Review Press, 1983. p. 148-65.

The author, senior lecturer at the Centre Universitaire Antilles-Guyane in Martinique, discusses the economic and political situation on Guadeloupe and Martinique from a world system Marxist viewpoint. Blérald's observations on island economic weakness, state of island cultural identity, and political sophistication show the functional and philosophical paradoxes of the Antillean situation and why a true independence movement, to which he is sympathetic, remains thwarted.

239 **Heading toward a new instability in the Caribbean's eastern tier?**
Scott B. MacDonald, Erik Kopp, Victor J. Bonilla. In: *The Caribbean after Grenada: revolution, conflict, and democracy.* Edited by Scott B. MacDonald, Harald M. Sandstrom, Paul B. Goodwin, Jr. New York: Praeger, 1988. p. 173-94.

Surveying the political climate in the French Caribbean in the mid-1980s, the authors treat Martinique in the framework of the entire French Caribbean and also put the French departments in a larger regional political context. They call attention to an increased polarization in island political expression and greater economic disequilibrium, both conditions that would point to increased political instability.

240 **Martinique and Morne-Vert: French "departmentalisation" or Caribbean "plantation economy"?**
William F. S. Miles. *Anthropology*, vol. 10, no. 1, p. 19-32.

Miles, a political scientist who worked in Martinique in the late 1970s and early 1980s, assesses the appropriateness of the Baber-Horowitz debate on the village of Morne-Vert. He first concludes that Martinique's is no longer an insular plantation-based economy, but one which is totally integrated into France's. Agriculture and related activities are no longer dominant features of the island economy. Miles proposes instead a 'bureaucratic economy', heavily dependent on subsidies from France. He further states that Baber's work does not put Morne-Vert in a Martinican perspective which, had it done so, would have shown how atypical the village is. Miles argues for a more empirical appreciation of both the village's and island's unique social and economic evolutions and for less theoretical refinement of time-specific descriptions.

241 **Martinique in transition: some implications of secondary modernization in a dependent society.**
Arvin W. Murch. *Revista/Review Interamericana*, vol. 7, no. 2 (1977), p. 207-15.

This article reviews France's 'artificial modernization of Martinique', revealed in island infrastructure, family planning, expanded public education and mass media, and government-subsidized migration to France. In the short run, Murch argues, social programmes and overall well-being may inhibit nationalism. Departmental status guarantees social and economic security for islanders; that security has caused Martinique's political left to abandon calls for autonomy from France and to substitute a call for autodetermination within the French system. This article is a continuation of Murch's earlier work *Black Frenchmen* (q.v.), but here, for the first time, he cautions about the 'reservoir of anger' that the island's dependence on France is provoking.

242 **Marxism at the crossroads: the political thought of Césaire and Fanon.**
John Gaffar LaGuerre. *Caribbean Studies*, vol. 15, no. 1 (1975), p. 84-93.

Discussing new critical books on Césaire and Fanon, this review article focuses on the uneasy alliances the two Martinican intellectuals had with French communism and socialism. LaGuerre explores their embracement of the French Communist Party and the intellectual left as inherently contradictory, because both were part of the establishment in white, imperial Paris.

243   **Mitterand's headache: the French Antilles in the 1980s.**
      Scott M. MacDonald, Albert L. Gastmann.   *Caribbean Review*,
      vol. 13, no. 2 (1984), p. 18-22.

Martinique's and Guadeloupe's political and economic situations have become more
and more dependent on France since departmentalization in 1948 and the authors here
briefly review their evolution. The negative balance of trade; the decline of the sugar
industry; the infusion of metropolitan investment, tourism and residents into the
islands; and welfare-type payments have contributed to an unbalanced economy. This
article states that the growing political unrest of the mid-1980s may be traced to an
artificial modernization of the islands and the lack of an effective, pro-independence
leader who could complete the process of decolonization. Instead, at the very time the
French government's policy was to promote autonomy or independence in the
Antilles, local resistance to and fear about independence have added a stronger French
military role to an already complicated and enigmatic dependency situation.

244   **Nationalism in the French Antilles: evaluation of Murch's thesis.**
      Roy L. Austin.   *Revista/Review Interamericana*, vol. 6 (1976),
      p. 102-04.

This paper is among the many that attempt to analyse and explain why the French
Antilles (Martinique and Guadeloupe) have remained departments of France while
virtually all of the former British West Indies have become independent. Austin cites
the theses of Arvin Murch and Jean Crusol regarding nationalist sentiment and then
spends the bulk of the paper discussing political representation, social inclusivism,
education and economic opportunity in the two groups of islands during the 1950s and
1960s. Austin concludes that the nascent nationalism which was present in all the
islands during the 1930s failed to mature in the French departments because of rapid
social and economic improvements after the Second World War.

245   **Political integration as an alternative to independence in the
      French Antilles.**
      Arvin W. Murch.   *American Sociological Review*, vol. 33 (1968),
      p. 544-62.

The author believes that Martinique and Guadeloupe were contradictions to the global
trend toward nationalism after the Second World War and that while other colonies
were achieving independence, these islands increased their political integration with
France. Murch attributes the lack of a strong nationalism in the islands to overall satis-
faction among leaders with the level of social equality. He proposes that the difference
between the French Antilles and the now-independent British Caribbean was the
former's closer and more advantageous political relationship with France. In this article Murch reports on surveys among local leaders which reveal a low level of
nationalist sentiment, a belief that independence was not feasible, and a 'romantic'
orientation toward France instead of toward local history and institutions. When combined with early universal suffrage and formal education, Murch believes these factors
have inhibited a viable nationalist movement.

246 **Political status of the French Caribbean.**
Gerard Latortue.   In: *Politics and economics in the Caribbean.*
Edited by T. G. Mathews, F. M. Andic.   Río Piedras, Puerto Rico:
University of Puerto Rico, Institute of Caribbean Studies, 1971.
p. 169-89.

This chapter details the administrative and legislative changes that occurred in
Martinique and Guadeloupe after departmentalization in 1948. It then scrutinizes those
favouring political autonomy from France, a distinct minority in the late 1960s, those
with objections to autonomy, and the position of the French government. The author
concludes that leaders favouring autonomy have never articulated in clear, precise
terms exactly what it would mean and thus autonomy remains a vague concept for
most French Antilleans.

247 **Regional reform in the French periphery: the overseas
departments of Réunion, Martinique, and Guadeloupe.**
Helen Hintjens.   *Regional Politics and Policy*, vol. 1, no. 1 (1991),
p. 51-73.

An historical background survey is provided of the French overseas departments as a
context in which to understand the regional reforms of the Mitterrand socialist government elected in 1981. The author concludes that there is a virtually universal desire in
the overseas departments to remain economically and legally integrated with metropolitan France. Desires for autonomy are largely confined to cultural and political
realms.

Administration

248 **L'espace regional martiniquais.** (Martinican regions.)
Christian Beringuier.   *Cahiers d'Outre-Mer*, vol. 20, no. 78 (1967),
p. 150-84.

The first section of this article examines Martinique by physical, demographic, and
economic regions, using data from the 1954 and 1962 censuses. It then synthesizes
these into seven 'homogeneous geographic' regions. The second section discusses the
urban framework of the island emphasizing the absolute primacy of greater Fort-de-
France over the small cities and bourgs that comprise regional administrative centres
on Martinique. Finally, the author proposes a 'rational' development structure for the
island. This article is a good example of the regional planning techniques and literature that came into vogue in the 1960s and 1970s. It proposes to redirect growth and
development, above all by public stimulation and incentives, thereby reducing the
deep regional imbalances affecting Martinique.

Economy

General

249 Agribusiness bourgeoisie of Barbados and Martinique.
Michael Sleeman. In: *Rural development in the Caribbean.* Edited
by P. I. Gomes. London: C. Hurst & Company; New York: St.
Martin's Press, 1985. p. 15-33.

Through interviews and colonial and metropolitan documents, Sleeman traces the
merging of once-separate mercantile and land-owning interests into the same hands on
Barbados and Martinique. This process gave rise to powerful new and local élites. In
Martinique this new bourgeoisie developed out of the oldest white creole planter families who, by taking advantage of French loans to transform the sugar industry, built
and acquired modern sugar factories in the late 19th century. Then, after the destructive eruption of Mont Pelée in 1902, the same handful of *Békés* opened new
commercial houses in Fort-de-France and came to dominate all aspects of
Martinique's economy – a monopoly that has been perpetuated by endogamy.

250 Basic data on the economy of Martinique.
Waltar Haidar. *Overseas Business Reports*, vol. 69, no. 26 (June
1969), 8p.

This is a succinct and still valuable description of Martinique's economy. Tables show
the destinations and values of prinicipal exports and imports and clearly demonstrate
Martinique's dependence in 1966-67 on French government salaries and subsidies to
its economy.

251 L'économie martiniquaise. (The Martinican economy.)
Eugene Revert. *Les Cahiers d'Outre-Mer*, vol. 1, no. 1 (1948),
p. 28-39.

Although brief this is a useful historical and contemporary survey of Martinique's
economy, which traces the fortunes of all agricultural products as well as ancillary

industries, particularly rum and brandy. Revert, who worked on Martinique during much of the 1940s, comments on the extreme economic polarization of the population, with perhaps two per cent controlling eight-five per cent of all exports and the vast majority of all imports to the island. However it is Revert's comments on the malnutrition and poverty of most Martinicans, the declining agricultural base, the rapid population growth, and the resulting economic and social paradoxes that make this paper important. Revert was an early and reliable observer of the issues and problems that have afflicted Martinique in the modern era; many of the more recent studies of island society and economy have emanated from his conclusions and his questions.

252 **The economy of the French Antilles.**
Roland Jouandet-Bernadat. In: *Politics and economics in the Caribbean.* Edited by T. G. Mathews, F. M. Andic. Rio Piedras, Puerto Rico: University of Puerto Rico, Institute of Caribbean Studies, 1971. p. 191-215.

Based on statistics from the early 1950s until 1961, this article shows the unbalanced, disjointed, and externally-oriented nature of the economies of Martinique and Guadeloupe. The socio-professional structure of Martinique is dominated by the primary (agricultural) and tertiary (service) sectors. Because there is so little industry, value-added or multiplier effects are extremely weak. The author unfavourably compares economic development on Martinique with that of Barbados. On an island faced with high population growth and the difficulty of creating local jobs, the author points to tourism, birth control, and migration as partial remedies, but he is not hopeful about early solutions to the islands' deep economic problems.

253 **Sugar and survival. The retention of economic power by white elites in Barbados and Martinique.**
Michael Allen. In: *Peasants, plantations, and rural communities in the Caribbean.* Edited by Malcolm Cross, Arnaud Marks. Guildford, England: University of Surrey, Department of Sociology and Royal Institute of Linguistics and Anthropology, Department of Caribbean Studies, Leiden, 1979.

This paper looks at the strategies of white élites to maintain economic dominance through traditional economic, social, and political sources of power and compares the élites of Barbados to the far more homogeneous and powerful Martinican planters. The sugar industry has long been declining on Martinique and most local cane is used in rum with refined beet sugar imported from France. *Békés* ran down sugar so they could invest in other, more profitable agricultural activities such as the protected post-Second World War banana industry. *Békés* have also increased their interest in the retail trade sector, a development simultaneous with increased transfer of public funds from France to Martinique. The author attributes the greater effectiveness of Martinican *Békés* to their great influence in French agricultural policy making.

French policy and Martinique

254 **Caribe francés: temores ante una major 'cercanía' europea.**
(French Caribbean: fears of the larger European community.)
Daniel van Eeuwen. *Nueva sociedad*, vol. 100, p. 40-49.
This article is an assessment of the ambiguities and contradictions of the situation in
the Caribbean overseas departments of Martinique, Guadeloupe, and Guiana. These
departments have become increasingly dependent on France: high salaries, subsidized
economies, and widespread unemployment render them ever more noncompetitive.
Reactions of prominent Caribbean political leaders are presented in the article, as are
the interests of France in maintaining a presence in the tropical Americas. This is a
useful summary of primary literature concerning political and economic events and
reactions in the overseas departments and in France during the late 1980s.

255 **Les départements français d'Amérique: Guadeloupe, Guyane,
Martinique face aux schémas d'intégration économique de la
caraibe et de l'Amérique latine.** (The French departments of
America: Guadeloupe, Guiana, and Martinique facing Caribbean and
Latin American economic integration schemes.)
Louis Dupont. Paris: L'Harmattan, 1988. 303p. maps. bibliog.
Dupont begins an economic analysis of France's three American overseas departments
by examining structural realities and the economic impact of tourism. In the second
section he looks at regional economic schemes, including the Caribbean Common
Market, and theories of economic evolution. In the final section he examines the actual
constraints and factors conditioning the economic status of the departments in light of
their being an integral part of France.

256 **Dual legacies in the contemporary Caribbean: continuing aspects
of British and French dominion.**
Edited by Paul Sutton. London: Frank Cass, 1986. 266p.
The papers in this volume focus on several aspects of slavery's legacy in the
Caribbean: the decline of the sugar industry; insularity and political fragmentation;
and the relationship between Creole culture and Europe. There are many references to
Martinique but two chapters specifically address Martinican issues. See M. Sleeman's
'Sugar in Barbados and Martinique: a socioeconomic comparison', p. 62-88 (q.v.), and
J. Crusol's 'An economic policy for Martinique', p. 188-200 (q.v.).

257 **An economic policy for Martinique.**
Jean Crusol. In: *Dual legacies in the contemporary Caribbean:
continuing aspects of British and French dominion.* Edited by Paul
Sutton. London: Frank Cass, 1986. p. 188-200.
This short chapter presents an assessment of the potential strengths and current weak-
nesses of Martinique's economic situation. The author then proposes a general
economic policy that is based around change in people's tastes, import substitution,
and decentralization.

258 **La Martinique, économie de plantation: un survol historique.**
(Martinique's plantation economy: an historical overview.)
Jean Crusol. *Les Cahiers du Centre d'Études Regionales Antilles Guyanes*, vol. 28 (1972), p. 3-31.
Crusol's article is a recapitulation of Martinique's economic history. It emphasizes the post-Second World War transformation of the island's economy from its traditional and local agricultural base to a new integration with and dependence on metropolitan expenditures and investments which are focused in the urban and public sectors.

259 **Martinique, its resources and problems.**
Christian Laigret. *Caribbean Commission Monthly Information Bulletin*, vol. 7, no. 8 (1954), 17p.
This brief article calls attention to the rapidly growing and increasingly marginalized Martinican population. Laigret laments the island's low and insufficient food production and problems resulting from high population density. The author, prefect of Martinique, proposes government-sponsored emigration to French Guiana, new enterprises such as fishing and cement factories, and tourism development as remedies for population pressure, low local income, and unfavourable trading conditions. This viewpoint, written in 1954, seems representative of those who have directed French policies toward the island.

260 **Sugar in Barbados and Martinique: a socioeconomic comparison.**
Michael Sleeman. In: *Dual legacies in the contemporary Caribbean: continuing aspects of British and French dominion.* Edited by Paul Sutton. London: Frank Cass, 1986. p. 62-88.
Shows how Martinican planters were able to gain control of all aspects of the sugar industry in the 19th century when other island economies were losing control to metropolitan financial interests. Martinique's economic élites have successfully commercialized other crops as sugar has declined in value. The author argues that the *Béké*'s strategic role in determining French economic policy for the overseas departments has allowed them to invest in the tourist industry, retail trade, and other high value export crops. But, as local opportunities for investment have declined, many *Békés* have both invested overseas and left the island as well.

Employment

261 **Labour conditions in Martinique.**
L. Debretagne. *International Labor Review*, vol. 32, no. 6 (1935), p. 792-800.
This article is a realistic description of jobs and work conditions in Martinique in the early 1930s from the vantage point of the head of the government's labour inspection service. He briefly reviews the status of workmen's compensation insurance, hours of work and the working week, and overall worker living conditions. He acknowledges that wealth was polarized in Martinique in 1935, that the island was among the most

expensive in the Caribbean, and that the trade union movement was not yet well developed.

262 **Note sur les revenus en Martinique.** (Note on revenues in
   Martinique.)
   Roland Bernadat-Jouandet. *Caribbean Studies*, vol. 4, no. 3 (Oct.
   1964), p. 14-31.

This short report examines sources of income in Martinique between 1956 and 1962. It includes tables that show data on the cost of living, luxury item imports, the cost of social services, and sources of income. Jobs, particularly functionary posts, are the number one source of income and growing rapidly; businesses and firms are the second largest source; social services and public sector benefits are the the the third largest group and growing rapidly; capital and property are a distant fourth. The strong growth in income between 1956 and 1962 was fuelled, the author believes, by large price increases in goods and rapid population growth.

Agriculture and
Natural Resources

263 Caribbean fishing and fishermen: a historical sketch.
Richard Price.   *American Anthropologist*, vol. 68, no. 6 (Dec. 1966),
p. 1363-83.

Examines the origins of Caribbean fishing techniques and subcultures, tracing their historical development among island Caribs, early French colonists, slaves, and freedmen. The author proposes that the strong independent nature and self-reliance in today's fisherfolk arose from the special socio-economic role their predecessors played in plantation society. Price maintains that fishing, in a manner similar to the trades and kitchen gardening, offered blacks a way out of the rigid plantation economy and endowed them with skills and some autonomy. This article focuses on the Lesser Antilles, with historical information drawn from reports of French visitors such as Labat, DuTertre, and Breton. The entire discussion pertains to Martinique and there are numerous specific references to the island.

264 Caribbean sugar industries: constraints and opportunities.
G. B. Hagelberg.   New Haven, Connecticut: Yale University, Antilles
Research Program, 1974. 173p. bibliog. (Occasional Papers, no. 3).

This volume is an important original and insightful overview of sugar industries in the Caribbean. The author argues against generalizations on Caribbean sugar production, documenting the large number of small landholders involved in it. He presents an array of statistics on sugar production, including many on Martinique, and evaluates their meaning and applicability. The text considers the economic effects and social costs of recent predictions and policies concerning regional sugar industries. Hagelberg argues that negative stereotypes regarding plantations, colonization, labour exploitation, and single-crop economies have all strongly influenced policies and trends during the 1960s and early 1970s. This is the best single source for understanding the regional sugar industry in the 1970s, and should be the starting point for a more detailed examination of the specific Martinican situation.

265 **Classification des essences forestières de la Martinique d'après leur utilisation.** (Classification of Martinican forest species according to use.)
Henri Stehlé. *Caribbean Forester*, vol. 3, no. 1 (1941), p. 29-31.

The author lists fifteen groupings of Martinican forest species, ranging from fine cabinetry woods and marquetry woods to tannins and dyewoods, firewoods, and woods for resins, glues, and gums.

266 **Current problems facing the peasantry in the north-east of Martinique.**
Maurice Burac. In: *Contemporary Caribbean: a sociological reader.*
Edited by Susan Craig. Trinidad and Tobago: published by the author and printed at the College Press, 1981-82. vol. 1/2, p. 383-403.

This chapter is a descriptive survey of farming in the north-eastern Capesterre district in 1969, supported with useful but undocumented statistics. Small farmers who own one to five hectares grow sugar and, increasingly, bananas, which at the time of the study were their chief source of revenue. Microfundia owners, the most numerous group of smallholders, farm about one hectare as a polycultural kitchen garden for home consumption and sale in local markets. Exodus to the urban areas of Martinique and the French metropolis by peasant landowners in all groups has resulted in increased 'mixed' farming, whereby owners also sharecrop the abandoned lands of others. Burac discusses types of tenancy and farming methods as well as the low profits and precarious living conditions that have long plagued all small farmers of this region.

267 **Désengagement paysan et sous-production alimentaire. Martinique. Marie-Galante, Barbade.** (Farmer disengagement and alimentary underproduction. Martinique. Marie-Galante. Barbados.)
Romain Paquette. Montréal: Les presses de l'université de Montréal, 1982. 212p. maps. bibliog.

A study of peasant agriculture, land use, crop selection, and food production which focuses on twelve properties in the districts (*quartiers*) of St. Joseph and Morne des Esses and is based on field work done in 1976-77. Paquette concludes that small, polycultural farmers are increasingly marginalized by agricultural research and policies originating in metropolitan France. These and general economic policies contribute to growing ecological, economic, and food instability in Martinique, whereby individual landowning families and the island as a whole lose their autonomy.

268 **Dooryard gardens of Martinique.**
Clarissa Kimber. *Yearbook of the Association of Pacific Coast Geographers*, vol. 28 (1966), p. 97-118.

This article examines the origins, floral composition, layout, management, and functions of three dooryard gardens in ecologically distinct rural areas of Martinique. Kimber regards the dooryard garden as a post-Emancipation development of individual landowners on small freehold plots. The gardens have multiple uses but their primary purpose seems to be the provision of food. They do not, however, fulfil all of the owners' food requirements. This article contains detailed maps of each of the three gardens and a table wherein each of the cited garden plants is classified botanically and by its intended use.

269   **La fin des plantations?** (End of the plantations?)
Raymond Massé. Montréal: Centre de recherches caraïbes, 1980.
150p.

Several research projects on rural change in dependent societies of the French Antilles are synthesized and summarized in this volume. It examines the Antillean heritage from the colonial past and the evolution since 1935 of landholdings, export structure, market gardening, and agricultural labour. It also considers the role and viability of small peasant farmers and plantation production in an increasingly interdependent global economy. Vauclin, a plantation community in the south, and Morne-Vert, in the northern highlands, are studied to trace the influence of recent land reform and agricultural reform laws as well as structural economic changes in the islands and France.

270   **Individualisme et traditions techniques chez le pêcheur**
Martiniquais. (Individualism and traditional techniques among Martinican fishermen.)
Jean Benoist. *Cahiers du Centre des Études Regionales Antilles-Guyane*, vol. 11 (1967), p. 47-63.

This article offers a general description of Martinican fishing: coastal fishing grounds; boats, especially canoes fashioned from a single gum tree; tools, including lines, nets, and hoops; and practices. In a concluding section Benoist discusses the extreme conservatism and independence characteristic of local fishermen. The total lack of cooperative efforts among them, while permitting great autonomy and minimizing risk for each individual, prevents capital accumulation and modernization of equipment and methods.

271   **Plan d'aménagement et d'exploitation rationnelle de la forêt**
martiniquaise. (Plan for management and rational exploitation of Martinican forests.)
Henri Stehlé. *Caribbean Forester*, vol. 3, no. 1 (1941), p. 32-38.

Although Martinique doesn't possess a true indigenous forest, because of widespread introduced species, it still possesses remnants worthy of study, management, and exploitation. Stehlé reports approximately 8,000 hectares (20,000 acres) of publicly owned forest on the island. This document outlines a plan of access, cutting, and reforestation for Martinique's forested areas.

Health and Medicine

272 **Géographie médicale de la Martinique.** (Medical geography of
Martinique.)
Etienne Montestruc. *Les Cahiers d'Outre-Mer*, vol. 2, no. 5 (1949),
p. 54-62.

This short article is a summary of the seasonal and regional distribution of diseases on
Martinique in the mid-1940s. The author pays particular attention to malaria, intestinal
parasites like hookworm and schistosoma, and typhoid fever. He sees the very uneven
seasonal and locational rainfall as the primary factor influencing pathology. Despite its
date, this is a useful historical survey.

273 **Médecine populaire à la Martinique.** (Popular medicine in
Martinique.)
Dan Bogden, Miriam Bogden. In: *L'archipel inachevé.* Edited by
Jean Benoist. Montréal: Les presses de l'université de Montréal,
1972. p. 233-48.

An introductory description of Martinican folk medicine is provided in this chapter; it
describes traditional systems of diagnosis, illness classification, illness etiology, and
treatment. All healers are associated with strong religious sentiments. Communication
with spirits and the saying of prayers accompany most remedies, which often involve
combinations of medicinal plants, baths, and modern pharmaceuticals. The authors
lament the loss of traditional pharmacopeia, many recipes of which are transmitted
orally.

Literature

Selected works of individual writers

Aimé Césaire

274 **Aimé Césaire, the collected poetry.**
Aimé Césaire, translated and with an introduction and notes by Clayton
Eshleman, Annette Smith. Berkeley, California: University of
California Press, 1983. 408p.

This volume contains more than 150 of Aimé Césaire's poems in French and in
English translation. There are six collections: notebook of a return to the native land
(1939); the miraculous weapons (1946); solar throat slashed (1948); lost body (1950);
ferraments (1960); and novea (1976). The translators write that they have assembled
works which connect Césaire to the mainstream of modern French poetry. They link
him to the masters of French modernism, particularly Rimbaud and Lautreamont, and
to surrealism. They see négritude, the expression of black culture that Césaire's work
has come to embody, and surrealism as having parallel goals. Césaire also displays an
extraordinary love for plants, the natural world, and Martinican commonfolk. His
work is characterized as demonstrating an unmatched prophetic authority, a mastery at
blending cruelty with tenderness, and a constant ability to surprise and delight – in
short, an artistic talent that combines both his vision and sense of history.

275 **Discourse on colonialism.**
Aimé Césaire, translated by Joan Pinkham. New York: Monthly
Review Press, 1972. 79p.

Written by the former communist Césaire, this political essay was first published in
1955. In it the author indicts Western colonialism as violent, racist, and barbaric, sur-
passed only by the capitalist barbarism of the United States. Césaire also includes as
enemies the intellectuals, journalists, and others who represent capitalism. He speaks
out about the virtues of non-European societies and their communal, democratic, and

fraternal natures. Césaire's denunciation of American and European hegemony and the suffering it has caused stops short of calling for complete separation from it or of violent revolution.

276 **Lost Body.** (Corps perdu.)
Aimé Césaire, introduction and translation by Clayton Eshleman, Annette Smith, illustrations by Pablo Picasso. New York: George Braziller, 1986. 131p.

Originally issued in 1950 as a limited edition, this book is a republication of a volume designed and specially illustrated by Pablo Picasso. Both poems and engravings are surrealistic and primitivist. The poems, full of earth and particularly island images and sharply punctuated word rhythms and phrases, are considered transitional, and more introspective, than Césaire's earlier work.

277 **Non-vicious circle: twenty poems of Aimé Césaire.**
Aimé Césaire, translated by and with introduction and commentary by Gregson Davis. Stanford, California: Stanford University Press, 1984. 121p.

Davis's objective is to present poems exemplifying fundamental aspects of Césaire's thought, imagery, and style as they crystallized into a coherent expression and philosophy in the late 1940s and early 1950s. The commentary analyses the poet's self-awareness and language as they came to embody the mythopoesis of négritude, an expression of the cultural elements and shared past of Martinican blacks and a literary resistance to the French colonial policy of assimilation.

278 **Return to my native land.**
Aimé Césaire, translated by John Berger, Anna Bostok, with an introduction by Mazisi Kunene. Harmondsworth, England: Penguin Books, 1969. 95p.

This is Aimé Césaire's first book-length and most well-known poem, written in 1939 about his imminent return to Martinique after eight years of study in France. It is in this poem that the word 'négritude' first appears prominently to express a distinct black identity and awareness. Césaire is thus credited with giving the name to a movement and ideology that he, Leopold Senghor (from Senegal) and Léon Damas (from French Guiana) had begun to articulate during their years together in Paris in the 1930s.

Frantz Fanon

279 **Black skins, white masks.**
Frantz Fanon, translated by Charles L. Markmann. New York: Grove
Press, 1967.
Fanon, a black psychologist born on Martinique and university-educated in France,
here sets forth a psychology of Martinique and, by extension, the entire French West
Indies. He discusses with blunt candor the role of the French and Creole languages in
cultural identity, interracial love and sex, the numerous complexes associated with
blackness and colonialism, and the self-conscious inferiority of blacks in Martinique
but not in mainland France. Fanon's proposed humanism, which he maintains to be
French (therefore white, civilized, manly, not inferior), is the only means of breaking
the power of these complexes and living with dignity and freedom. Fanon's life
became an embodiment of the cultural, racial, and psychological confusion he
expresses here.

280 **A dying colonialism.**
Frantz Fanon, translated from the French by Haakon Chevalier and
with an introduction by Adolfo Gilly. New York: Grove Weidenfeld,
1967. 181p.
This is an amazing book about the Algerian revolution for independence from France,
written in 1959 before freedom was achieved. It is amazing because Fanon, a black
Martinican, writes here with passion as an Algerian advocating peasant/worker revolt
and violent struggle against colonial and white European dominance. This volume
became a classic among revolutionaries in Africa and Latin America and Fanon
became a revolutionary hero. In his blanket reflection on and condemnation of French
colonialism and his praise of Algerian courage and non-Western culture, Fanon never
once mentions his colonial Martinican origins and his own true racial identity.

281 **Wretched of the earth.**
Frantz Fanon. New York: Grove Press, 1963. 255p.
Fanon, the Martinican-born psychiatrist, undertakes here a thorough historical and
psychological analysis of colonialism; he sets forth many of the inherent conflicts
between national élites, political parties, and the need for order on one hand, and peasants, a national consciousness, and violence on the other. He discusses the
unpreparedness of most national middle classes to run a new country and points out
that an economy and society will often be judged by criteria left from the colonial
period. A neo-colonialism, with political and economic order maintained by dictator-
ship, will often be the result and peasants will remain oppressed. Fanon cites the
complicit role of intellectuals who continue to function in the European sphere. He
warns of the great differences between social and economic conditions when
European countries achieved national unity and those of present-day underdeveloped
areas. More vital than a choice between capitalism and socialism, between development and under-development, is the need to redistribute wealth on a massive basis.
Now thirty years old, this book remains a brilliant and prescient analysis of the problems of development, the conflict between colonizer and colonist, and the gap between
élite and peasant. Fanon utterly rejects Europe as the place to look for any solutions at
all.

Patrick Leigh Fermor

282 **The violins of Saint-Jacques.**
Patrick Leigh Fermor. New York: St. Martin's Press, 1977. 139p.
This novel is set on the fictitious islet of Saint-Jacques and concerns the life of the privileged white squirearchy. The story culminates on the night of a grand masked ball in the elegant city of Plessis, when the volcano Salpetrière erupts and kills all the inhabitants. The book is a recreation of the society of St. Pierre and the night that Mont Pelée erupted in 1902. Fermor is not a native of Martinique, and is more well-known as a British officer in the Mediterranean theatre than as a novelist.

Robert Gaillard

283 **Marie of the isles.**
Robert Gaillard, translated from the French by Merle Severy. New York: A. A. Wyn, 1953. 422p.
This historical novel romanticizes the lives and love story of French nobleman Jacques du Parquet, first governor and builder of the colony of Martinique, and his wife-to-be, Marie Bounard de Saint-André. In the course of this story many of the events in 17th-century Martinican history are presented.

Edouard Glissant

284 **Caribbean discourse: selected essays.**
Edouard Glissant, translated and with an introduction by Michael Dash. Charlottesville, Virginia: University Press of Virginia, 1989. 272p.
Consists of the talks, papers, and poems written between 1962 and 1981 on the wide range of subjects that have always interested Glissant: the Creole language; colonialism; economic dependence; dispossession; migration; race and négritude; cultural evolution; and the Caribbean collective consciousness. In several instances Glissant outlines, diagrams, or summarizes all of Martinique's history in a few words, lines, or images. Yet the themes in this book are sweeping and universal; in it Martinique's land and people become a prism through which to view and review the world. Glissant's words speak of a painful past and an uncertain future, of uneasy marriages in Martinique's cultural and environmental spaces. The lyricism and penetrating self-awareness that permeate these essays communicate a cautious, and at times weakened, hope and resiliency about Creole Martinique and, by association, Caribbean society as a whole.

285 **Culture et colonisation: l'équilibre antillais.** (Culture and
colonization: the Antillean equilibrium.)
Edouard Glissant. *Esprit*, vol. 30, no. 305 (1962), p. 588-95.

Glissant writes of the abdication of a collective spirit among French-speaking
Antilleans, pointing out that they see themselves as French not Antilleans. He indicts
the colonial system that before and after emancipation moved individuals among the
Antilles, Europe, and the African colonies, causing depersonalization and unclear loy-
alties. There has been an ongoing Balkanization in the Antilles, with each of the
islands relating more closely to North America or to European countries than to each
other. With each component of the Antillean population looking elsewhere for orientation and reward, there has been no synthesis of all the region's cultural elements into a
unique and sustainable Antillean character or identity.

286 **Monsieur Toussaint.** (Mister Toussaint.)
Edouard Glissant, translated by Joseph G. Foster, Barbara A. Franklin,
introduction and notes by Juris Silenieks.   Washington, DC: Three
Continents Press, 1981. 129p. bibliog.

This play by Martinican Edouard Glissant is about the Americas' first authentic black
hero, Toussaint L'Ouverture, the slave who led the successful rebellion against France
in Haiti. Its four parts are entitled 'the gods', 'the dead', 'the people', and 'the
heroes'; all are set in Santo Domingo in two simultaneous time frames, that of
Toussaint's prison term and that of insular space. This is a most nonconventional play.
In it Glissant attempts a prophetic vision of the past by use of Antillean folklore and
consciousness, interaction between the dead and the living, and linguistic codes to
convey class and distance.

287 **The ripening.** (La lézarde.)
Edouard Glissant, translated and introduced by Michael Dash.
London: Heinemann, 1985. 195p.

This prize-winning first novel is based in Martinique during the post-war elections of
1945. It is a fictionalized account that bears some resemblances to Glissant's own participation in Aimé Césaire's overwhelming election as mayor of Fort-de-France that
year. The Lézarde River, which runs down from the island's rugged mountain interior
to the sea, symbolizes the political maturation of eight young islanders, the emergence
of their collective political will, and their struggle as individuals and as a society to
win self-respect. Glissant's writing is always probing the Caribbean consciousness and
is laden with symbolism and references to the Martinican landscape. Martinique's cultural and environmental duality is represented by the rugged interior hill lands and the
naïve, driven, and individualistic former maroons living there contrasted with the con-
taminated coastal plains which are inhabited by victimized, lazy, and worldly former
slaves.

Louise Locquet-Bellemare

288 **Une martiniquaise sous le drapeau.** (A Martinican serves her
country.)
Louise Locquet-Bellemare.   Paris: La Pensée Universalle, 1974. 321p.
Humorously written, this book is concerned with a young woman's schemes to leave
Martinique and go to the 'Mother Country' of France in 1948, just after departmentalization. Naïvely, she enlists in the army, and begins to discover the disagreeable
obligations of being French when that country's other colonies are engaged in wars of
independence with her.

René Maran

289 **Batouala.**
René Maran, translated by Barbara Beck, Alexandre Mboukou,
introduction by Donald E. Herdeck.   London: Heinemann, 1973.
149p.
This novel by Martinique-born René Maran, who became an employee of the French
colonial service and worked in several French African colonies, is set in Ubangui-
Shari, part of French Equatorial Africa. The story, told from the African point of view,
marks a turning point in the style of West Indian writers toward articulation of a new
black cultural identity and for its denunciation of colonial injustices. The story concerns a Banda chief named Batouala, one of his wives, and a rival. There are
descriptions of tribal customs, such as a circumcision and excision ceremony; the recognition of and adherence to ancestral wisdom and tradition, burial rites, and beliefs;
and expression of African attitudes toward the French colonizers, their poll tax, and
cultural customs. *Batouala* is among the first novels written by an Afro-Caribbean to
tell a black's, and not a French or imitative French, story and it both received the pre-
stigious Goncourt prize and caused a scandal for its boldness and break with tradition.

Mario Mattioni

290 **Ma nou l'esclave.** (Ma nou, the slave.)
Mario Mattioni.   Fort-de-France: Éditions Desormeaux, 1986. 157p.
This romance is historical fiction set in the earliest days of the French occupation of
Martinique. The main characters are du Parquet, the first French governor of the
island; Ma Nou, the first African slave in the colony; and Severin, stripped of his
native American culture after being transformed into a Carib warrior. The author,
Mario Mattioni, is a well-published ethnologist and has set this work in the meeting of
the three distinct peoples who have given shape to Martinique's present-day cultural
legacy.

Joseph Zobel

291 **Black shack alley.** (La rue cases-négres.)
Joseph Zobel, translated and introduced by Keith Q. Warner.
Washington, DC: Three Continents Press, 1980. 184p.

An autobiographical narrative, this novel tells the story of a young black growing up in Martinique between the two world wars. José, the narrator, begins with his early childhood being reared by his hard-working grandmother in a poor, ramshackle village attached to a sugar plantation. She ensures that he obtains a primary education at a nearby resident school, where his awareness of social inequalities and the value of education in escaping poverty are born. He wins a scholarship to the lycée in Fort-de-France, and the scene shifts to the urban environment, where José's mother works as a maid. *Black Shack Alley* deals with many of the themes pertinent to a black Martinican childhood: the predominance of women in family life; the separate spheres of island blacks and whites; the classic French educational system so ill-tailored to Martinican reality; and the great poverty of most island blacks.

Anthologies

292 **Black poetry of the French Antilles.**
Translated by Seth L. Wolitz. Berkeley, California: Fybate Lecture Notes, 1968. 37p.

This short publication contains translated poems by Martinican poets Aimé Césaire, Gilbert Gratiant, and Etienne Léro as well as works by poets from Haiti, Guadeloupe, and French Guiana.

293 **From the green Antilles, writings of the Caribbean.**
Edited by Barbara Howes. London: Granada Publishing, 1971. 397p.

Five Martinican writers are represented in this collection of short stories, poems, and excerpts. In addition to a selection by the well-known Aimé Césaire, it also includes the short stories 'The gift', by Joseph Zobel; 'Up in smoke', by Clement Richer; 'Elisa the hustler', by Pierre Duprey; and 'Calderon's revolt', by Raphael Tardon.

294 **Green cane and juicy flotsam.**
Edited by Carmen C. Esteves, Lizabeth Paravisini-Gebert. New Brunswick, New Jersey: Rutgers University Press, 1991. 273p.

Twenty-seven short stories by Caribbean women writers are brought together in this volume which is intended to illustrate the broadest spectrum of themes, styles, and techniques in contemporary feminist short story writing. Jeanne Ayvrard, who spent part of her youth in Martinique, is represented by a story depicting the alienation and exile of a Caribbean woman in Paris. All the stories somehow touch the unique and painful experiences of class, race, sex, and migration that so permeate the lives of Antillean women.

295 **The négritude poets, an anthology of translations from the French.**
Edited by Ellen Conroy Kennedy. New York: The Viking Press,
1975. 284p. bibliog.

This volume, which is an historical and social as well as literary treatment of
négritude, is divided into three sections, the first of which is 'Caribbean poets in
French'. Martinican poets whose work is included are: René Maran, whose style is a
precursor to négritude; Aimé Césaire, here represented by an abridgement of 'Notes
on a return to the native land' and six other poems; and Edouard Glissant, with
excerpts from his prose poem 'The Indies'. The volume itself is valuable because it
situates black West Indian poets, who were long overlooked as being minor voices,
among their contemporaries in Africa and the Indian Ocean. It examines the themes
and stylistic influences and currents that have run throughout 20th-century black
poetry, linking French-speaking writers with earlier Harlem Renaissance writers and
finally with British-African and Caribbean poets.

296 **Negro poets of the French Caribbean. A sampler.**
Norman R. Shapiro. *The Antioch Review*, vol. 27, no. 2 (1967),
p. 211-28.

This article is a look at the rise of an authentic black poetic voice in the French
Caribbean, with translated poems from the 1930s to the 1960s. While the article
presents works from the entire region, of special interest here is the discussion of the
pioneering role of little-known Martinican poet Etienne Léro. 'Nausea', by Auguste
Desportes of Martinique, is included as an example of the rare expression of discon-
tent with the overall human condition by a French-Negro poet, as distinguished from
the more race-specific bitterness of most black French writers of that time.

Literary criticism and history

297 **African presence in Caribbean literature.**
Edward Kamau Braithwaite. In: *Slavery, colonialism, and racism.*
Edited by Sidney W. Mintz. New York: W. W. Norton & Company,
1974. p. 73-109.

Braithwaite organizes the African element in Caribbean writing along a four-part continuum, which he categorizes as follows: first, the theoretical presence wherein Africa
is expressed in a vague and romantic way – only an imperfectly understood desire;
second, the African survival, in which local folk traditions with evident roots in Africa
are expressed but not explicitly traced to Africa; third, the African expression, wherein African rhythms, word-plays, chants, and improvisations are incorporated into the
written literary tradition; and finally, the literature of reconnection, in which African
elements in the Caribbean are directly and intentionally linked to the continental
'heartland'. Braithwaite uses writings from the French-, Spanish-, and English-speaking Caribbean traditions in this quite useful typology of the regional literature.

298 **Afro-French writers of the 1930s and creation of the negritude school.**
Edward A. Jones. *CLA Journal*, vol. 14, no. 1 (Sept. 1970), p. 18-34.

The author of this article was studying in Paris during the 1930s and there met Aimé Césaire and Leopold Senghor, two of the three poets he writes about here. Césaire's poetry he characterizes as beautiful and sophisticated, although it often expresses anger and bitterness and describes what is ugly. It is Césaire, Jones writes, who first puts forth the heritage of African origins and colonial injustices which all blacks share.

299 **Black writers in French, a literary history of negritude.**
Lilyan Kesteloot, translated by Ellen Conroy Kennedy. Philadelphia: Temple University Press, 1974. 401p. bibliog.

This now-classic work was the first synthesis and is still the essential starting place for research into the 20th-century black awareness and cultural movement called négritude. It systematically examines the precursors of négritude, who include Martinicans René Menil and René Maran; the birth and definition of négritude; négritude's earth poets and poetry; Second World War writings and political activities; and post-war French-language writers, publications, cultural identity, and literary directions. Martinican writers Gratiant, Menil, Zobel, Glissant, Fanon, Aimé Césaire, Suzanne Césaire, and Maran are all extensively cited and discussed, as is the role of island culture and milieu. This volume was originally published as a doctoral thesis in 1961.

300 **The crisis of identity: studies in the Guadeloupean and Martiniquan novel.**
Frederick Ivor Case. Sherbrooke, Québec: Éditions Naaman, 1985. 190p.

This volume is concerned with the meaning of social realism as expressed in Martinican and Guadeloupean literature. After an initial discussion of social realism, the author examines the ideological evolution, the themes of alienation and the absurd, and aesthetic experimentation in the body of work of three Caribbean authors. In one chapter Edouard Glissant's four novels are discussed as an experiment in aesthetics and social consciousness, which reveal a progressive pessimism in their observations on Caribbean society. Throughout this volume other Martinican and Caribbean writers are discussed in relationship to both social realism and the principal authors under consideration.

301 **French West Indian background of 'Negritude'.**
G. R. Coulthard. *Caribbean Quarterly*, vol. 7, no. 3 (Dec. 1961), p. 128-36.

The author examines négritude as a neo-African art form or literature. His conclusion, based on writings of the West Indian founders of the school, is that the style and literary terms of writers like Fanon, Gratiant, Damas, and Roumain are European or Western and developed in a distinctly French context. Only Aimé Césaire, Coulthard proposes, develops a new poetic and uniquely Caribbean style.

302 **Guadeloupe et Martinique: la difficile voie de la Négritude et de l'Antillanité.** (Guadeloupe and Martinique: the difficult road of Négritude and Antilleanity.)
Jacques Corzoni. *Presence Africaine*, vol. 76, no. 4 (1970), p. 16-42.

Demonstrated here is how the search for an authentic black identity has been led by Caribbean writers like René Maran, Léon Damas, Aimé Césaire, René Menil, Frantz Fanon, and Edouard Glissant. Whereas their vision has been seized and politically implemented in Africa, it has never become shared by a large number of black West Antilleans. The author proposes that until négritude as a black cultural conscience is fully embraced by most Guadeloupeans and Martinicans, there will be no possibility for liberation in the islands.

303 **Histoire littéraire de l'Amerique française des origines à 1950.**
(Literary history of French America from its origins to 1950.)
Auguste Viatte. Québec: Presses Universitaires de France, 1954.

An opening chapter in this basic general history of French-language writings in the Americas considers the colonial milieu and authors in the16th and 17th centuries. The bulk of the volume is comprised of chapters on regional literature, each written in a chronological manner. One of these is devoted to Lesser Antillean writers, of whom Martinicans comprise the majority. Some poetry is included in the text and an index of names of all mentioned authors is useful. A concluding chapter looks at historical trends in French-American writing, intra-regional influences in style, and the robustness of the literature being written by French-speaking Americans at mid-century.

304 **An introduction to the French Caribbean novel.**
Beverley Ormerod. London: Heinemann, 1985. 149p.

This small volume is an analysis of common themes and objectives in 20th-century French Caribbean literature. Ormerod sees Aimé Césaire's *Notebook of a return to my native land* as beginning a tradition which is followed by the six novels discussed here. All deal with the social injustice, repressive colonial legacy, and dual sense of alienation that Césaire sets forth in *Notebook*. Ormerod analogizes the original fall into slavery, current black alienation, and hopes for future deliverance with Biblical themes about the fall from paradise and the search for and journey to a promised land. She sees the plantation and plantation life as representing the fall and captivity and some protagonists as accepting that paradise, or escape, cannot be attained and consequently learning to survive in hardship. Ormerod also proposes that the heroes in the novels are redeemers coming to save the oppressed. She argues that French West Indian novelists have long been judged critically by sociological and political criteria and not on their literary and creative merits. In addition to Césaire, this book is concerned with Martinicans Joseph Zobel and Edouard Glissant, although numerous other Martinican authors are included in the discussion.

305 **Literature and ideology in Martinique: René Maran, Aimé Césaire, Frantz Fanon.**
   F. A. Irele.   Buffalo, New York: State University of New York at Buffalo, Council on International Studies, 1972. 35p. (Special Studies, no. 16.)

Irele here traces the development of a new social consciousness in Martinique through the writings of Maran, Césaire, and Fanon. He sees a single progressive evolution of ideological awareness resulting in the elaboration of a worldview. He believes the ideologies emanating from the black world contain a certain basic unity in that they were called into existence by the encounter between Europe and Africa. The three Martinican writers studied here have, with other African-Americans, turned to Africa in search of a meaning for the collective contemporary black experience.

306 **Marvellous realism – the way out of negritude.**
   Michael Dash.   *Caribbean Studies*, vol. 13, no. 4 (1974), p. 57-70.

Dash believes that négritude could not have been a literature that led the way to psychological and political emancipation for Caribbean blacks because it was so concerned with the past and protest. Négritude failed because it was too rooted in and connected with the white colonial European civilization against which it was protesting. Dash proposes that it is not in their alienation as slaves or as the colonized that blacks find creative energy, but in their own myths, legends, and oral traditions. Their imaginations provide the energy and vigour of Third World peoples and give expression to a need and desire for continuity, survival, and renascence. Dash also believes that whereas poetry was the means that best expressed protest, it is the novel that best serves as the means to express a new and positive creative energy.

307 **Myth and history in Caribbean fiction.**
   Barbara J. Webb.   Amherst, Massachusetts: The University of Massachusetts Press, 1992. 185p. bibliog.

This volume is a critical examination of three contemporary West Indian novelists, Alejo Carpentier, Wilson Harris, and Martinican Edouard Glissant. According to Webb, these three share the view that folk traditions arising from the encounter of Africans, Amerindians, and Europeans in the Caribbean are a primary source of historical understanding and artistic innovation. For all three writers the distinction between novelist and historian is an unclear, perhaps meaningless one. Webb examines their novels under three broad themes: the relationship between folk imagination and history; the quest for origins and the myth of El Dorado; and the dialectics of culture wherein history becomes mythic discourse. For Glissant, she says, myth both preserves and creates history and he uses folk traditions to explore cultural identity, world view, and historical reality. This volume is an illuminating demonstration and discussion of how myth and history come together in the works of these Caribbean writers and how they have contributed to an awareness of a common historical and cultural legacy for the entire region.

308 **Negritude: an annotated bibliography.**
   Colette V. Michael.   West Cornwall, Connecticut: Locust Hill Press, 1988. 315p.

The strength of this excellent bibliography lies in the vast number of secondary publications that deal with the evolution, definition, scope, and direction of négritude as a movement and a literature. The primary sources, anthologies and bibliographies included were selected from the nearly 500 annotated secondary sources. There are many references to Aimé Césaire, Frantz Fanon, and Edouard Glissant. The volume is a good starting place for research on Martinican cultural identity, literature, and writers.

309 **Négritude in the feminine mode: the case of Martinique and Guadeloupe.**
Clarisse Zimra. *Journal of Ethnic Studies*, vol. 12, no. 1 (1984), p. 53-77.

Zimra writes of négritude as a literary movement and ideology born of specific histori-cal circumstances, defined by socio-political reality of the 1930s, but whose transformations and consequences extend into current literature. Women writers, always part of the movement, have been overlooked. Zimra examines the writings of feminist Francophone authors who, she contends, have enriched the evolving vision of négritude by writing about the 'double patriarchal jeopardy' women suffer, first as negresses and second as females. The work of Martinican novelist Marie-Magdaleine Carbet is discussed as being representative of an early, milder generation of female négritude writers. Zimra attributes the generally less strident writings of Martinicans to a better socio-economic ambience there than exists on Guadeloupe. Whether life for the average Martinican is indeed better is not defensible, but the island's comparative prosperity is widely cited and assumed.

310 **La négritude: un second souffle?** (Negritude: A new inspiration?)
Martin Steins. *Cultures et Développement*, vol. 12, no. 1 (1980), p. 3-43.

In this article négritude is analysed as an ideology that enfolds and articulates such vital contemporary issues as black African civilization and culture, the black 'soul', nationhood, race, and the union of all these factors. As the post-colonial experiences of blacks in Africa and the Americas have diverged, négritude has been modified and diversified. While this scholarly treatment primarily examines the writings and thought of Senegalese poet and politician Leopold Senghor, it is an important philo-logical analysis of the evolution of négritude thought and political reality.

311 **Novels on the French Caribbean intellectual in France.**
Merle Hodge. *Revista/Review Interamericana*. vol. 6 (1976), p. 211-31.

This article reviews four novels of exile written in France, two of which are written by Martinique-born writers. René Maran's *Un homme pareil aux autres* (A man like other men) is about a Martinique-born man who strongly identifies with France and the French values he has lived under for most of his life. He is sent as a colonial adminis-trator to Africa, where he demonstrates compassion toward Africans, but is not revolutionary. In this novel Maran does not show the cultural awakening so evident in other négritude writers. Joseph Zobel's autobiographical *La fête à Paris* (Party in Paris) is permeated by a discussion of race and colonialism. A peasant schooled in Martinique, Zobel went to France at the age of thirty-one, and his novel exhibits racial pride but also fraternity between blacks and whites. The French in Zobel's books embody French liberalism, particularly with regard to black colonies and black people. Zobel idealizes the French and French behaviour as well as the relationship between intellectual black men and white women. Hodge demonstrates how these novels reveal the distinct emotional ties the French West Indian had for France, a reflection of the French policy of assimilation. The 'colonial' in these novels exists always in relation to France and French culture.

312 **Resistance and Caribbean literature.**
Selwyn R. Cudjoe. Athens, Ohio: Ohio University Press, 1980. 319p. bibliog.

What makes this a valuable contribution to Caribbean literary criticism is the way in which the author integrates and analyses the French, English, and Spanish literature together as forming a distinctive Caribbean tradition. Cudjoe uses the novel to link the development of a mature regional literary form with the passage from dependence and dispossession to democracy, 'manhood,' and independence. In this insightful, comprehensive study, which is the outgrowth of a doctoral dissertation, the works of Césaire, Fanon, and Glissant are discussed at length.

313 **Righting the calabash: writing history in the female Francophone narrative.**
Clarisse Zimra. In: *Out of the kumbla: Caribbean women and literature*. Edited by Carole Bryce Davies, Elaine Savory Fido. Trenton, New Jersey: Africa World Press, 1990. p. 143-59.

This scholarly overview examines the gradual development of female mulatto characters and a female voice with perspective in Francophone Caribbean literature. It reflects on the genealogical and gender awareness of major male négritude writers like Fanon and Césaire. In recent writings by women, female lineage becomes the means through which ancestral wisdom and connections are passed in Caribbean society. The silent, ever-present mother has become a new voice in Caribbean literature and a counterpoint to the untrustworthy male, who is preoccupied with territory and pre-slave African origins.

314 **Voices of negritude.**
Edward A. Jones. Valley Forge, Pennsylvania: Judson Press, 1971. 125p.

The poems and commentary in this volume are intended to demonstrate the message and range of style among the early négritude writers of the 1930s and 1940s. All demonstrate the consciousness of colour, racial pride, and unity of all blacks from sharing a history of oppression, poverty, and injustice. One short chapter is devoted to Aimé Césaire's epic lyrical poem *Cahier d'un retour au pay natal*, which is seen as the most eloquent, yet scathing expression of black suffering and identity.

315 **"Le voyage et l'espace clos" – island and journey as metaphor: aspects of woman's experience in the works of Francophone Caribbean women novelists.**
Elizabeth Wilson. In: *Out of the kumbla: Caribbean women and literature.* Edited by Carole Boyce Davies, Elaine Savory Fido. Trenton, New Jersey: Africa World Press, 1990. p. 45-57.
This chapter examines women as they are portrayed by female French Caribbean novelists. It concludes that the concerns of alienation, identity, isolation, and escape are almost universally present among female protagonists. For those characters who look within, the enclosed island space is secure and protective, the women fulfilled. For others, particularly those who entwine their lives with white Frenchmen, the island becomes a prison. These two themes represent the two identities with which the French Antilles in general struggle.

316 **Women writers of the French-speaking Caribbean: an overview.**
Marie-Denise Shelton. In: *Caribbean women writers: essays from the first international conference.* Edited by Selwyn R. Cudjoe. Wellesley, Massachusetts: Calaloux Publications, 1991, p. 346-56.
The author attempts to isolate thematic currents and to identify narrative practices that allow an identification of the feminine literary imagination in novels by women writers from Martinique, Guadeloupe, and Haiti. She finds that they utilize themes of alienation, the desire for oneness, and the call for a transformation of structures and values that destroy freedom. Shelton finds that the preoccupations and perspectives of French-speaking women authors are every bit as diverse as those of male writers and that women writers are just as fully engaged in the experiences and aspirations of Caribbean peoples.

Criticism of individual writers

Aimé Césaire

317 **Aimé Césaire.**
Lilyan Kesteloot. Paris: Éditions Pierre Seghers, 1962. 207p.
Some fifty complete poems are included in this small volume on Césaire. Kesteloot, now a highly regarded Belgian philologist, writes an excellent commentary on Césaire and his work. She demonstrates how it is impossible to separate Césaire's literary work from his racial and cultural heritage and his political views and activities. His surrealist poems, perhaps the fullest expression of early negritude writings, are characterized by the powerful and vivid use of African symbols, Creole West Indian images, and flawless, dazzling French.

318 **Aimé Césaire: black between two worlds.**
Susan Frutkin.   Miami: University of Miami, Center for Advanced
International Studies, 1973. 66p.
This tiny volume is based on a master's thesis submitted to the University of Miami in
1968. It is as much about Martinican political history between 1940 and 1971 as it is
about Aimé Césaire, since the two are quite intertwined. This is a good basic overview, based primarily on secondary sources and Césaire's writings, of his relationship
with Marxism and the French Communist Party, on his views concerning departmentalization and Martinican nationalism, and on the island's underdevelopment and need
for political autonomy. The ironies and paradoxes in many of Césaire's beliefs and
attachments are pointed out, particularly his commitment to the French parliamentary
system and to France itself.

319 **Engagement and the language of the subject in the poetry of Aimé
Césaire.**
Ronnie Leah Scharfman.   Gainesville, Florida: University of Florida
Press, 1987. 133p. (Humanities Monograph no. 59.)
Originally written as a doctoral dissertation at Yale University, this is the most recent
criticism published in English on Aimé Césaire's poetry. It is a thoroughly academic
monograph and not the best place to first approach Césaire's oeuvre. The study,
together with *Modernism and negritude*, by A. James Arnold, and *Aimé Césaire, the
collected poetry*, translated and annotated by Clayton Eshleman and Annette Smith, is
evidence of the high critical regard and literary importance Césaire and his writings
have achieved. This particular volume has as its singular objective the simultaneous
analysis of Césaire's complex and therefore inaccessible literary forms and his dualis-
tic colonial identity. It is this paradoxical combination which has long contributed to a
limited appreciation and incomplete analysis of Césaire's writing.

320 **Modernism and negritude. The poetry and poetics of Aimé
Césaire.**
A. James Arnold.   Cambridge, Massachusetts: Harvard University
Press, 1981. 318p.
In this scholarly volume Arnold attempts to jointly examine the two legacies and con-
stituencies of Aimé Césaire's considerable body of published poems: the ideological,
with its themes of liberation and négritude; and the surrealistic, with its ambiguous
images and obfuscating modernism. The author, in a chronological study of Césaire's
poems, tries to demonstrate that complete revolution is unacceptable to Césaire and
that poetry was for him the means by which the painful contradictions between the
ideal and reality could be expressed.

321 **Un poète politique: Aimé Césaire.** (A political poet: Aimé Césaire.)
François Beloux.   *Magazine Litteraire*, vol. 34 (Nov. 1969), p. 27-32.
This is among the better interviews with Aimé Césaire. He talks at length about the
deep psychological alienation and cultural assimilation of black Martinicans and about
his own Marxist beliefs and political activities, his deep love for Haiti and the resulting plays he wrote on two of its heroes, and his belief in the basic unity of all blacks.

Frantz Fanon

322 Fanon.
Peter Geismar. New York: The Dial Press, 1971. 214p.

Here is the definitive general biography on Frantz Fanon. Geismar believes that all of Fanon's original ideas evolved out of his own life and experience. This account thus discusses his life chronologically, weaving his professional accomplishments and political ideas into the narrative. Fanon, a black from Martinique, studied medicine and psychiatry in France and later practised in Algeria and Tunisia. He was a brilliant administrator and visionary in hospital reform. It was in Algeria that he became a political revolutionary, indeed a leader in that colony's war for independence against France. Fanon's writings of the late 1950s, which resulted from that experience, became near manifestos for Third World anticolonial movements and for all black power militants. This book, based on many interviews with Fanon's family, friends, and colleagues, contains details and insights that come from Geismar's study, not only of Fanon's life, but also of the Algerian Revolution.

323 Frantz Fanon, a critical study.
Irene L. Gendzier. New York: Pantheon Books, 1973. 300p.

At the time of writing this was the fourth biography on Fanon, and was intended to be a new critique of his writings and their most important themes. It is divided into four sections: his family circumstances and intellectual roots in Martinique and France; an analysis of his writings in psychiatry; a study of his militant years in Tunisia and Algeria; and finally, a critical look at his role and legacy in Third World revolutions. In contrast to others who have studied the life of Fanon, Gendzier proposes that he never forgot his past or Martinican home country. She attempts to show that one can only understand his late political writings and revolutionary activities in the Algerian struggle for independence in the context of his life of personal struggle for a clear psychological, racial, cultural, and political identity. The book draws heavily on previous accounts of Fanon's life and work as well as on interviews with family and associates. It is both a thorough synthesis and original interpretation.

324 Frantz Fanon and the psychology of oppression.
Hussein Abdilahi Bulhan. New York: Plenum Press, 1985. 299p. bibliog.

This biography of Fanon is among the most recent and is perhaps the most systematic in its approach to his life and psychology. The author sympathetically presents Fanon as a black psychiatrist who wrote and lived to intentionally affect the history of racism and colonialism. In contrast to earlier biographies, this focuses specifically on Fanon's legacy as a psychologist and his theories on oppression and violence and their manichean groundings. The book is an ambitious attempt to fit Fanon's life, philosophy, and writings into the considerable sociological, psychological, and psychiatric literature on race, mental illness, colonialism, and violence. It is a work particularly useful for psychologists and sociologists studying the developing world or otherwise victimized people. The author's discussion of Fanon's contribution to colonial psychiatry and to a psychiatry of personal and social liberation is noteworthy.

325 **Holy violence: the revolutionary thought of Frantz Fanon.**
B. Marie Perinbaum. Washington, DC: Three Continents Press, 1982.
182p. bibliog.
Literature on Martinican Frantz Fanon, his life, and his writings is huge and continues
to grow. This biography, which focuses on Fanon's concepts of creative conflict and
counterviolence, attributes a larger role in his revolutionary thought to his Martinican
youth than most earlier studies. The author attempts to show the continuity and overall
cohesion of Fanon's thought, which first developed as creative conflict in Martinique,
turned to violence during his first years in Algeria, and evolved to holy violence by the
late 1950s. Perinbaum analyses Fanon's philosophy for its contribution to the literature on both conflict resolution and tropical decolonization.

326 **The impossible life of Frantz Fanon.**
Albert Memmi. *The Massachusetts Review*, vol. 14, no. 1 (Winter
1973), p. 9-39.
Along with Fanon, the writer of this article, an eminent Tunisian psychologist, made
freedom from France in North Africa a personal work. Both he and Fanon also
explored the influence of oppression on the psychological and cultural expression of
the oppressed. When Fanon went to work as a psychiatrist in Algeria he totally identified himself as French, but while he was there he became transformed into an Algerian
and joined the struggle against France. Fanon did not consider himself black, but totally assimilated. Memmi writes of the uniqueness of Fanon's situation – fighting the
oppressor in the name of another, while never embracing the négritude of his own
teachers and former colleagues or his own West Indian origins. Alone among
Martinican intellectuals, however, Fanon was ready for a complete break with France.
Memmi sees Algeria assuming the place of Martinique in Fanon's identifications; it
became the ideal place for his neuroses. Fanon's death from cancer at the age of thir-
ty-six 'froze him ... as a prophet of the Third World, a romantic hero of
decolonisation'. This is a probing, insightful article.

327 **Myth and reality in the negro; in memory of Frantz Fanon.**
Gonsalv Mainberger. *Presence Africaine*, vol. 18, no. 46 (1963),
p. 211-24.
The author, a Dominican priest and specialist on African philosophy, has written this
homage to Frantz Fanon's life, ideas, and generally misunderstood proposals for the
future of African and Latin American peasants. He speaks of the inseparable nature of
Fanon's life and writings and of his need to experience and live out all the ambiguities, pain, and violence he felt about his race, colonial status, and psycho-sexual self.
Mainberger sees Fanon as an 'event', a living paradox and the first real champion of
the Third World peasant, which explains the many repercussions of his writings.
There are hints here of the yet-to-be articulated liberation theology, in Mainberger's
comments on what Fanon has to say to spiritual missioners.

328 **Parrot or phoenix? Frantz Fanon's view of the West Indian and
Algerian woman.**
B. Marie Perinbaum. *Journal of Ethnic Studies*. vol. 1, no. 2 (1973),
p. 45-55.
Examines Fanon's incomplete studies of two types of women: the bourgeois
Martinican who assimilated to the colonial system and the Algerian Arab woman who

he incorrectly believed rebelled against it. Fanon's assessment was that the bourgeois Antillean, through cohabitation, education, and behavioural norms, tried to whiten herself. His work, however, never extended to peasant and working-class women, who comprise the majority of Martinican society.

Edouard Glissant

329 Beyond negritude: some aspects of the work of Edouard Glissant.
Beverley Ormerod. *Contemporary Literature*, vol. 15, no. 3 (Summer 1974), p. 360-69.

This scholarly article explores Edouard Glissant's rendering of African and European worldviews as they are relevant to the Caribbean present. Ormerod proposes that Glissant's writings go beyond the anti-white, anti-European language of early négritude writers to celebrate the new cultural synthesis and multiracial society of the West Indies. Instead of being preoccupied by black-white dualism, Glissant advocates the embracing of a *métis* (mixed) way of life which is uniquely and recognizably Caribbean and that sets the region apart.

330 A caribcentric view of the world: the novels of Edouard Glissant.
Lauren W. Yoder. *Caribbean Review*, vol. 10, no. 3 (Summer 1981), p. 24-27.

In this review article attention is drawn to the use of the land-water relationship in Glissant's first two novels, *La lézarde* (The awakening) and *Le quatrième siècle* (The fourth century). Yoder links earth imagery with what it communicates about slave and maroon lifestyles, worldviews, and identity. Water images, employed when characters interact with the river and sea, relate more to a growing self-awareness and political awakening. Both earth and water, she asserts, are elements of creation and hope in Glissant's novels, and symbolically point to a new, and island-centred Martinican (and Caribbean) identity.

331 'Comment peut-on être Martiniquais?' The recent work of Edouard Glissant.
Richard Burton. *The Modern Language Review*, vol. 79, pt. 2 (April 1984), p. 301-12.

This article reviews the four novels of Edouard Glissant, *La lézarde, Le quatrième siècle, Malemort*, and *La case du commandeur*, and *Caribbean discourse*, a volume of essays, in which he reconstructs and indeed creates the island's black history. The author discusses the two traditions of black Martinique – the slave, a plantation dweller, and the maroon, a rebel and hill dweller – in which Glissant frames island society. Glissant's reality is a far more complex one, involving more political, economic, and cultural threads than that of the early négritude writers who confined themselves to simple European and African images. Glissant's first two novels, which ended with departmentalization just after the Second World War, are optimistic and forward-looking. The later novels are backward-looking and quite pessimistic, with the characters unsure of their ancestry and who they are. This personal imbalance in the novels' characters echoes the distortions in the entire island landscape, culture, and economy that are discussed in *Caribbean discourse*.

332 **Discourse and dispossession: Edouard Glissant's image of contemporary Martinique.**
Beverley Ormerod. *Caribbean Quarterly*, vol. 27, no. 4 (1981), p. 1-12.

The author distils and reviews Glissant's 1981 books *Caribbean discourse* and *The driver's hut*, in which he treats the ambivalent Martinican sense of identity. The lack of an official folk history that embraces the pain and humiliation of slavery or the bravery and independence of marronage has combined with French policies of assimilation to weaken Martinicans' nationalistic sentiments and bonding with and stewardship of their land. As islanders have increasingly accepted the French way of life – consumerism, language and 'charity' – they are unable to embrace the past they share with Caribbean neighbours. That neither Martinique nor France recognizes the distinct cultural and environmental heritages of the two, perpetuates Martinique's *ennui* and non-productive dependence on the metropolis. Glissant, in both books, reveals his vision of a future identity for Martinicans and a unity and integration of the island with its Caribbean neighbours.

333 **Edouard Glissant: the novel as history rewritten.**
Vere Knight. *Black Images*, vol. 3, no. 1 (Spring 1974), p. 64-85.

This article discusses Edouard Glissant as the French Caribbean writer who, along with Berthène Juminer, should be credited with rehabilitating the past of the French Caribbean black. Knight here discusses Glissant's first two novels, *La lézarde* and *Le quatrième siècle*. The latter begins with the painful crossing of a slave ship from West Africa to Martinique and then follows two families through the island's early history until emancipation and ultimately into their places among the many divisions of class and colour that characterize Martinican society. *La lézarde* is concerned with the political participation of young blacks in 1945 and their role in electing a black to the French Assembly and in shaping island history. Knight sees Glissant's objective in using novels to create a history as two-fold: first, to teach and inform black Martinicans about their own long-denied and suppressed history; and second, to remove and heal the psychological shame connected with this horrible and painful past of enslavement and colonization.

334 **Glissant's prophetic vision of the past.**
Juris Silenicks. In: *African literature today. II. Myth & history*.
Edited by Eldred Durosimi Jones. London: Heinemann, 1980.
p. 161-68.

Three novels by Edouard Glissant are analysed, with the author seeing in them Glissant's attempt to build a regional identity, a task calling for the interpretive ability of an historian and the creativity of a poet. Glissant's works, Silenicks says, are absorbed in historical time, but the past derives its meaning from the future – from the region's potential. Caught between past and future is the present, which is full of pain, uncertainty, and a sense of helplessness and aimlessness. Glissant, whose writing is complex and inaccessible, remains, to a certain extent, a prophet without a country, for his work has found a readership primarily in France and he is little read in the Caribbean.

René Maran

335 **René Maran.**
Keith Cameron.   Boston: Twayne Publishers, 1985. 176p.

This biography is the first book in either French or English to be devoted entirely to René Maran, the Martinican-born writer whose pioneering role in the development of an authentic black French literature has only recently been acknowledged. Maran served for thirteen years between 1910 and 1923 in tropical French Africa in the colonial service, but spent the remainder of his life in France as a writer and journalist. His many writings have the common objective of furthering an understanding of black peoples and he was the earliest writer to incorporate African peoples and customs into his stories. As a precursor to the more well-known négritude writers, Maran occupies a unique place among black French writers; he writes of his discomfort with his own black skin, of the destructive effects of colonialism in Africa, of his embrace of and identification with the French language and culture. His writings contain none of the revolutionary and political ideology of later writers. This sympathetic biography argues rather that Maran needs to be evaluated in the context of the specific period in which he lived and wrote. Cameron believes Maran's prolific writings can now be properly appreciated from a literary standpoint and also as valuable social and historical documents for the years prior to the Second World War, decolonization, and the black power movement.

Arts and Folklore

Art

336 **Two painters of the tropics: Lafcadio Hearn and Paul Gauguin.**
Mary Louise Vincent. *Caribbean Studies.* vol. 10, no. 3 (1970),
p. 172-81.

This paper examines the work of Hearn and Gauguin in Martinique against the accounts that view them as modern primitivists and rather simplistic rebels against material bourgeois values. Vincent proposes that the visit of each to Martinique in 1887 marked a professional turning point. Gauguin's work thereafter began to show the strong colours, unusual angles, and light skies that constituted a definitive break with Impressionism. Hearn's sketches and word-pictures, though still impressionistic, began to show detailed variety of both atmospheric conditions and daily life of the local people. This demonstrated his versatility and a heretofore perhaps too-easily dismissed sensitivity.

Folk arts

337 **The cooking of the Caribbean islands.**
Linda Wolfe, the editors of *Time-Life Books.*   New York: Time-Life
Books, Foods of the World, 1970. 208p.

Part of Time-Life's exceptional Foods of the World series, this volume is a classic. It is still the most accessible and complete all-round introduction to the crops, foods, cuisines, and recipes of the Caribbean islands. It contains numerous photographs and textual references to Martinique and a dozen specifically Martinican recipes.

338 **Les derniers potières de Sainte-Anne, Martinique.** (The last potters
of Sainte-Anne, Martinique.)
Noëlle de Roo Lemos.   Montréal: Université de Montréal, Centre de
Rechérches Caraïbes, 1979. 75p.

Describes the pottery-making techniques of the Sainte-Anne commune on the
southwest coast of Martinique. Pottery-making is a woman's activity, and ceramics
are made in coils. As this traditional fishing village is linked more and more to the
money economy, the number of potters is declining and metal utensils are becoming
far more common. The author discusses the hypothesis that these potters represent a
continuation of pre-Columbian techniques. This is a well-illustrated paper, with many
diagrams and photographs of pots. The socio-economic aspects of pottery making are
also considered.

Magic

339 **Fishing rites and recipes in a Martiniquan village.**
Richard Price.   *Caribbean Studies*, vol. 6, no. 1 (April 1966), p. 3-31.

Fishing in Martinique, which is highly individualistic and self-sufficient, involves
nine major methods, each of which incorporates specific technologies and rituals.
This article reports the magic practices of Martinican fishermen in one village in
1963. It includes long lists of plants and pharmaceuticals used in fishing magic and
describes numerous rituals like beatings, purificatory baths, and the placement of
charms and medallions on canoes. The author discusses the origins of fishing magic,
proposing that Carib influences are much stronger than was generally accepted at the
time of his study. His tracings indicate that the earliest colonists began to synthesize
useful plants and practices of the Caribs with traditional French pharmaceuticals to
produce a unique local pharmacy that has only recently shown signs of being eroded
because of licensing regulations originating in France.

340 **La magie antillaise.**
Eugène Revert.   Paris: Annuaire International des Français d'outre
mer, 1977. 203p.

This volume constitutes a wide-ranging, descriptive survey of Martinican magic
(quimbois), carried out in 1949. The author recognizes that many traditional practices
were being strongly altered by French medicines and methods or were disappearing
altogether. This account covers rites and festivals (holidays); remedies, prescriptions,
and charms; potions, prayers, bewitchments, and countercharms; premonitions,
predictions, and tricks of sorcerers; and zombies, apparitions, and vodun. Revert
briefly discusses the origins and syncretism of Martinican magic and includes the
recipe notebook of a quimbois among the appendices. This volume is anecdotal,
without traceable accounts or data and is more a preliminary sketch or overview than
a definitive study.

341 **Magie et pêche à la Martinique.** (Magic and fishing in Martinique.)
Richard Price. *L'Homme*, vol. 4, no. 2 (1964), p. 84-113.

Using ethnographic data from the fishing hamlet of Belle-Anse in southeastern
Martinique, Price attempts to understand the relationship between danger and
uncertainty in fishing and magic and other ritualistic practices used by fishermen. He
elaborates a hierarchy of fishing methods according to danger and uncertainty and
then examines the rituals that accompany these methods. In a village characterized by
great individualism, Price looks at the contribution of ritual to social levelling when
any given fisherman is extremely lucky or, on the other hand, quite unfortunate. Line
fishing, done on the high sea, is the most dangerous, potentially the most lucrative,
and accompanied by the most ritual. Price's discussion is shaped within the
framework of Malinowski's theory of magic elaborated from fishing rites among
Trobriand islanders.

Music and dance

342 **Creole music and dance in Martinique.**
William K. Gallo. *Revista/Review Interamericana*, vol. 8, no. 4
(Winter 1978-79), p. 666-70.

Gallo discusses two styles of the *biguine*, the unofficial national dance of Martinique.
The bélé, a rural choral dance with a predominantly African style, is performed by a
double column or a circle of couples and accompanied by a drum. Music begins with
a phrase from the solo singer, part of which is repeated by the dancers. The St. Pierre
style involves a mixture of African, French, and American musical elements
performed by an orchestra, singer, and couples. Dances in this urban-popular tradition
include biguines, mazurkas, waltzes, and polkas. North American influences such as
drum sets and improvisations are attributed to the vigorous triangular trade between
Paris and New Orleans, by way of St. Pierre, Martinique, in the 19th century.

343 **Le danse aux Antilles: des rythmes sacrés au zouk.** (Dance in the
Antilles: from sacred rhythms to zouk.)
Jacqueline Rosemain. Paris: L'Harmattan, 1990. 90p.

This volume comprises a history of dance songs and rhythms in the Caribbean. The
author emphasizes the importance of calendas; ceremonial dances with African
origins but which are also heavily influenced by the Roman Catholic church.
Calendas later influenced the biguine, tango, rumba, and zouk. Martinique, in particular, is a locus for the development of many of these songs and dances.

344 **On interpreting popular music: zouk in the West Indies.**
Jocelyne Guilbault. In: *Caribbean popular culture*. Edited by John
A. Lent. Bowling Green, Ohio: Bowling Green State University
Popular Press, 1990. p. 79-97.

Zouk is a popular music of Martinique, Guadeloupe, Dominica, and St. Lucia,
important in the daily life of the Creole-speaking populations there. Zouk is a
Martinican word referring to parties at which the greatest freedom of expression is

allowed and it thus symbolizes the role of music in popular culture. After a general consideration of how musical experiences are affected by mass media, migration patterns, and folk culture, the author examines the narrative structures of zouk and how composers use music to connect the social, political, and musical environments. Guilbault considers zouk as a social force, with its message of emancipation, social harmony, and cultural identity. She speculates on the possibilities of zouk as a factor in the regional integration of Creole-speaking peoples and its role in giving identity to both expatriate and resident islanders – a role she perceives to be quite different from that served by reggae.

345 **Musique aux Antilles. Mizik bô kay.** (Music in the Antilles.)
Maurice Jallier, Yollen Lossen. Paris: Éditions Caribéenes, 1985. 147p.

Popular music in Martinique, Guadeloupe, and French Guiana is treated in this volume. Short chapters on such topics as the evolution of a distinctive French Antillean music, exterior influences on this music, and musical traditions are interspersed with chapter-long interviews with well-known music personalities who have developed new styles and popularized trends. A chapter on the Antillean song contains many examples with words in both Creole and French, followed by explanatory notes. The books closes with a survey on the role of music among young Antilleans.

346 **La musique dans la société Antillaise 1635-1902. Martinique, Guadeloupe.** (Music in Antillean society, 1635-1902. Martinique. Guadeloupe.)
Jacqueline Rosemain. Paris: Éditions l'Harmattan, 1986. 184p. bibliog.

The thread that ties this volume together is that of the three still-extant musical expressions of the French Antilles, present since the first days of European invasion: the drum, the biguine, and the quadrille. This thread has led the author through the political and folk history of the islands to examine the role of church, state, and folk groups and of African and European music. She ends the study with the destruction of the city of St. Pierre in 1902, since that city had been the centre of Martinican cultural life and of the biguine, the musical form that most characterizes Martinican music. This musicology of the islands contains the scores of many hymns, marches, songs, and anthems for each historical period. Of particular interest are the variations in both music and verses between France and the islands, and from island to island. This is a useful resource on Martinican music.

347 **Zouk: world music in the West Indies.**
Jocelyne Guilbault with Gage Averill, Edouard Benoit, Gregory Rabess. Chicago: University of Chicago Press, 1993. 279p. bibliog. disk.

This volume is a fine critical and historical study of the hot new dance music called zouk, written by the well-known ethnomusicologist Jocelyn Guilbault. The book examines the musicological and cultural aspects of zouk, which now pervades popular culture on Martinique and nearby islands but has also spread as far as Africa and Europe. In three parts, the book looks at the following: the island milieu and origins of zouk, which is sung in French-based Creole; the relationship between zouk and other Caribbean music styles such as the biguine and the cadence-lypso; and finally, the lyrics and choreography of zouk and the role the music plays in people's lives. The volume comes with a compact disk of fifteen songs recorded in the islands over a thirty-year period.

Stories and lore

348 **Contes de mort et de vie aux Antilles.** (Stories of death and life in the Antilles.)
Edited and translated by Joëlle Laurent, Ina Césaire. Paris: Nubia. 248p.

Twenty-two creole folktales were collected orally in Martinique and Guadeloupe and are presented in this volume. An introduction treats the Antillean storytelling tradition, the psychological and social roles represented by characters, and the themes and symbolism of the stories. Each story is published in both Creole and French, and there is a short section on transcription, syntax, and phonology. There are groups of sorcerers' tales, erotic tales, animal stories, and stories on the deeds of Ti-Jean, the mythical protagonist of many Creole Caribbean tales.

349 **Folk-lore of the Antilles, French and English. Part I.**
Elsie Clews Parsons. New York: American Folk-Lore Society, 1933. 521p. (Memoirs of the American Folk-Lore Society, vol. 26.)

This volume represents an invaluable and unsurpassed collection of tales, riddles, songs, proverbs, and verses from the Lesser Antilles and Haiti, collected between 1924 and 1927. The author writes in her preface that the richest fields for the folklorist in the Caribbean are the French islands or those islands which were once French and where 'French Creole' is still spoken. Some ninety-five tales from Martinique, many with music, are written up in Creole and French.

350 **Humor and riddles in Martiniquan folk literature.**
Michael M. Horowitz. *Midwest Folklore*, vol. 9, no. 3 (Fall 1959), p. 149-54.

Several Martinican stories are contained in this brief article, wherein self-ridicule is expressed through the use of Creole and French, sexual norms, and skin colour. There is also a section of riddles told during wakes. Horowitz proposes all these folk traditions as sources of anthropological information.

351 **A note on canoe names in Martinique.**
Richard Price, Sally Price. *Names*, vol. 14, no. 3 (Sept. 1966), p. 157-60.

Some 105 canoe names, collected from two villages on Martinique's southern coast, are grouped under saint's names, other religious names, proper names, ship names, other secular names, and initialled (unspelled-out) names. The authors suggest studies of the significance of such names by ethnographers.

Arts and Folklore. Stories and lore

352 Story-tellers of Martinique.
Elodie Jourdain. *Monthly Information Bulletin* (published by the Caribbean Commission), vol. 7, no. 12 (July 1954), p. 265-66, 268.

The author, who grew up on Martinique, briefly writes and reminisces about storytelling sessions there during her childhood in the late 1800s. She describes riddles, the repertoire of stories each storyteller possessed, and the songs and choruses that were interspersed with each story and sung by the audience. She attributes tales with animals and evil to Africa, those with fairies, knights, and wizards to Europe, and calls attention to the value of oral tradition and its preservation.

353 Word/song and nommo force in two black francophone plays: Simone Schwartz-Bart's 'Son beau capitaine' and Ina Césaire's 'Mémoire d'isles'.
Sandra Adell. *Journal of Caribbean Studies*, vol. 8, no. 1-2 (1990), p. 61-69.

Mémoire d'isles, written by Martinican Ina Césaire, is a series of monologues in which two elderly Martinican women reminisce, using Carnaval as the means through which they tap their memories. Although they speak in French, they make constant reference to their native Creole language.

Archives

354 Conseil souverain de la Martinique (Série B) 1712-1791.
Inventaire Analytique. (Supreme council of Martinique. [B Series].
1712-1791. Analytical inventory.)
Liliane Chauleau.   Fort-de-France: Archives Departementales de la
Martinique, 1985. 400p.

As representatives of the king the Supreme Council of Martinique was responsible for
administering justice on the island. This resource guide first describes its
composition, function, and competence. The bulk of the volume is a descriptive
analytical inventory of the registers of all court meetings and transactions between
1712 and 1791. It contains a complete index of persons mentioned, places, laws, and
subjects of laws. This is an invaluable guide to the records in island archives for the
student of 18th-century Martinique.

355 Guide des archives de la Martinique. (Guide to the archives of
Martinique.)
Liliane Chauleau.   Fort-de-France: Archives Departementales de la
Martinique, 1978. 72p.

Included in this useful volume is an introduction to Martinique's archives, its
contents, accessibility, and history. One chapter elaborates historical sources and
contents in the island's national archives arranged chronologically by period. A final
chapter briefly categorizes communal, diocesan, hospital, and private archives on the
island. The author is the director of Martinique's archival services.

Research guide to Central America and the Caribbean.
See item no 377.

Periodicals

356 Caribbean Affairs.

Port of Spain, Trinidad and Tobago: Trinidad Express, 1972- . quarterly.

This literary and political quarterly features topics of interest throughout the Caribbean Basin. Articles are authored by Caribbean writers for people in the region; this is a good source for Caribbean views.

357 Caribbean Contact.

Bridgetown, Barbados: Caribbean Contact. 1972- . monthly.

This publication is an ecumenical newspaper sponsored by the Caribbean Conference of Churches. It has excellent coverage of island politics, especially as concerned with human rights, church issues, and workers and labour unions.

358 Caribbean Geography.

Kingston, Jamaica: Longmans, Jamaica, 1983- . bi-annual.

Appears in two issues annually and is dedicated to the advancement of geography in the Caribbean. Articles range across geography and include the environment, culture, agriculture, planning, and land use. Each issue contains book reviews and a section on geographical education in the Caribbean classroom.

359 Caribbean Insight.

London: The West India Committee. 1978- . monthly.

This twelve-page monthly bulletin is devoted primarily to the economic and trade issues of the British Commonwealth Caribbean. The news briefs section has occasional pieces on the French Caribbean. The high abstention rate in the three French-Caribbean departments during the referendum on the Maastricht Treaty was reported in the November 1992 issue.

360 **Caribbean Quarterly.**
   Mona, Jamaica: University of the West Indies. 1949- . quarterly.
One of the objectives of this scholarly journal is to offer to West Indians 'reliable reading on their own history and culture [and on] social developments in the Caribbean'. Issues include research from the social and behavioural sciences, new poetry, stories, folktales, and drama, and book reviews and literary criticism. Notable writers such as Derek Walcott have been among the frequent contributors.

361 **Caribbean Review.**
   Miami, Florida: Caribbean Review, 1969- . quarterly.
This quarterly magazine is devoted to the Caribbean, Latin America, and their emigrant groups living abroad. Articles cover the arts, literary criticism, and a range of cultural, political and economic subjects. Each issue also contains book reviews and short stories. Most articles are written by academics and well-known novelists.

362 **Caribbean Studies.**
   Río Piedras, Puerto Rico: University of Puerto Rico, The Institute of Caribbean Studies, 1961- . quarterly.
A quarterly journal, this is devoted to the social sciences in the Caribbean and circum-Caribbean areas. It publishes regular current bibliographies that include general works on the French-speaking Antilles as well as entries for Martinique in particular. This is a good source for recent publications.

363 **Journal of Caribbean Studies.**
   Lexington, Kentucky: The Association of Caribbean Studies. 1980- . bi-annual.
Concerned with topical issues in the multi-lingual Caribbean. Issues are often focused on one broad topic; specific recent issues have been on the environment, the Caribbean and Europe, and the French Caribbean.

364 **Social and Economic Studies.**
   Mona, Jamaica: University of the West Indies, Institute of Social and Economic Research, 1953- . quarterly.
This is an important, refereed scholarly journal devoted to social scientific and historical research on Caribbean topics.

Reference Sources

365 **Amerindians of the Lesser Antilles: a bibliography.**
Compiled by Robert A. Myers. New Haven, Connecticut: Human
Relations Area Files, 1981. 158 leaves. map.

The objective of this bibliography, with its more than 1,300 entries, is to facilitate
knowledge of and access to the widely scattered and linguistically diverse literature
on indigenous peoples of the Lesser Antilles. Entries are grouped under the following
five categories: archaeology and prehistory; archives, history, travel and description,
and social science research; languages; biology, nutrition, and medicine; and
literature. The bibliography includes a geographical index, in which Martinique
shows more than 100 entries, and an author index. Depositories are indicated for most
referenced materials.

366 **Biographical dictionary of Latin American and Caribbean
political leaders.**
Edited by Robert Alexander. Westport, Connecticut: Greenwood
Press, 1987. 505p. bibliog.

The dictionary is an alphabetical listing by name, with a brief biographical sketch, of
the most important 19th- and 20th-century political leaders in Latin America and the
Caribbean. Aimé Césaire and Victor Sablé, with their political affiliations and
activities, are the Martinicans included.

367 **The Caribbean. 1975-80. A bibliography of economic and rural
development.**
Compiled by Manuel J. Carvajal. Metuchen, New Jersey: Scarecrow
Press, 1993. 894p.

Dissertations and publications are included for all Caribbean islands except Cuba and
Puerto Rico for the years 1975 through 1980, with the objective of providing a broad-
based point of departure for documents on economic and rural development. The
listed materials are considerably more eclectic than the title suggests and only a very

few entries are annotated. Two chapters are of interest to the student of Martinique, that on the Caribbean in general and that on the French Overseas Departments. Of the sixty-seven entries listed under the subheading of Martinique, six are doctoral dissertations on some aspect of Aime Césaire's oeuvre – a testimony to the remarkable recent interest in his writing. The general index is by subject, author, editor, and persons and institutions as subjects.

368 Caribbean Basin Databook, 1992.
Washington, DC: Caribbean/Latin American Action, 1991. 399p.
This annual databook is produced for investors, businesspeople, and policymakers and is published by a private-sector organization that actively influences international trade policies and business activity in the region. The seven pages on Martinique include an economic summary, trade, tax, and financial incentives, banking service information, economic indicators, communication and transportation information, and a list of trade contacts.

369 Caribbean women novelists. An annotated critical bibliography.
Lizabeth Paravisini-Gebert, Olga Torres-Seda.   Westport, Connecticut; London: Greenwood Press, 1993. 427p.
A comprehensive listing of Caribbean women novelists and their work is provided in this welcome recent volume. Each entry is annotated. Marie-Magdaleine Carbet and Mayotte Capezia are among the most prolific of the seventeen Martinicans included, although none of their work is available in English. The number of Caribbean women writers is increasing rapidly and many of those cited here are still actively writing. This valuable resource work, with its hundreds of entries, attests to both the size of the literature and the growing interest in the female perspective.

370 Caribbean writers, a bio-bibliographical critical encyclopedia.
Edited by Donald E. Herdeck.   Washington, DC: Three Continents Press, 1979. 943p. bibliog.
An outstanding reference work, this is divided into four sections, the second of which is devoted to Francophone literature from the Caribbean. It contains an essay on the literature of the French Antilles and a list of more than eighty writers from Martinique. All of these are represented by capsule biographies and definitive lists of their book-length works as well as their more important pieces published in periodicals. This is an invaluable resource.

371 The complete Caribbeana, 1900-1975: a bibliographic guide to the scholarly literature.
Compiled by Lambros Comitas.   Millwood, New York: KTO Press, 1977. 4 vols.
These volumes are the requisite starting place for any social, biological, or physical science work in the Caribbean. The collection is now becoming a bit dated, particularly for the social sciences, in which research and literature have mushroomed in the last twenty years.

372 **Dictionary of contemporary politics of Central America and the Caribbean.**
Edited by Phil Gunson, Greg Chamberlain, Andrew Thompson. New York: Simon & Schuster, 1991. 397p.

This useful dictionary contains ten entries specifically related to Martinique, a map, and entries for other islands and political movements that relate to Martinique.

373 **Dissertation abstracts international.**
Ann Arbor, Michigan: University Microfilms. 1969-present.

Contains abstracts of dissertations available on microfilm or as xerographic reproductions for virtually every PhD-granting discipline. This is a useful source of information because many dissertations are never formally published as monographs or scholarly articles. Although dissertations in the humanities and social sciences written prior to 1980 are listed in other reference sources in this bibliography, for more recent dissertations on Martinique – and there are many, particularly in literature and literary criticism – *Dissertation Abstracts International* is the only up-to-date reference. It is available in most research libraries.

374 **A guide to Latin American and Caribbean census material. A bibliography and union list.**
Edited by Carole Travis. Boston: G.K. Hall, 1990.

This bibliography contains a section on Martinique (p. 416-27), compiled by L. Dethan and S. M. Rockett. The earliest entries in the list are included for historical reasons but are not proper censuses. Martinique began to enumerate its population from the earliest settlement, apparently to keep track of slaves, but these are not considered reliable figures. Only since 1954 has census-taking been carried out under the auspices of INSEE of the French government. Depositories in England are given for most entries.

375 **Historical dictionary of the French and Netherland Antilles.**
Albert Gastmann. Metuchen, New Jersey: Scarecrow Press, 1978. 162p.

This is a useful little volume for the English-speaking user interested in the socio-economic history of the French and Netherland Antilles. It is comprised of three nonduplicative sections on general information, the French Antilles, and the Netherland Antilles and includes Martinican place-names, authors, lists of governors, acronyms, terminology, and historical events. More than 150 of the entries in the first two sections of the volume will be useful to the student of people, places, and events of Martinique.

376 **Latin America and the Caribbean. A critical guide to research sources.**
Edited by Paula H. Covington. Westport, Connecticut: Greenwood Press, 1992. 924p.

An important interdisciplinary undertaking, this volume is a guide to research and bibliographical sources on the Caribbean and Latin America. It is organized around twenty-one topics that include dance, databases, geography, several periods of history, literature, and women's studies. Introductory essays survey the evolution of each topical discipline, current research trends, and the principal points of entry into the literature. These essays are followed by an annotated bibliography of reference sources and descriptions of specialized resources available in various libraries. With more than 6,000 entries, this is a major work and includes both contextual material for any study on Martinique and a number of references specifically on the French Caribbean.

377 **Research guide to Central America and the Caribbean.**
Edited by Kenneth J. Grieb. Madison, Wisconsin: University of Wisconsin Press, 1985. 431p.

A conference on Latin American history during the 1970s was the impetus for this book. Its intentions are two-fold: to identify and serve as a guide to major archival depositories, providing basic information about holdings, the type and scope of the sources, and hours and conditions for use; and to explore future directions for research and gaps in current knowledge. Two chapters are of particular interest to students of Martinique: 'The French West Antilles', by René V. Achéen (p.284-88), reviews historical studies, indicating the paucity of historical research, particularly in social history. He suggest numerous areas for future work. 'Martinique', by Liliane Chauleau, (p. 315-17), provides information about the Archives of Martinique in Fort-de-France. Chauleau briefly describes holdings from the last quarter of the 17th century until the present and mentions church records, judicial records, land records, vital statistics, and the Registry of Mortgages.

378 **Selected black American, African, and Caribbean authors. A bio-bibliography.**
Compiled by James A. Page, Jae Min Roh. Littleton, Colorado: Libraries Unlimited, 1985. 388p.

While primarily concerned with African-American literature of the United States, this reference work contains entries on Martinicans Aimé Césaire, Frantz Fanon, Edouard Glissant, and René Maran. Each entry includes a biographical sketch, a complete listing of fiction and non-fiction books published in English in chronological order, selected comments on the writer's career, and sources consulted and quoted.

379 **Theses on Caribbean topics 1778-1968.**
Compiled by Enid Baa. San Juan, Puerto Rico: University of Puerto Rico Press, Institute of Caribbean Studies, 1970. (Caribbean bibliographic series, no. 1.)

This bibliography covers master's theses and doctoral dissertations on Caribbean topics completed in French and English at United States universities. Disciplines covered include behavioural and social sciences, agriculture and natural sciences, education, the arts, and literature. There are thirty-two entries dealing specifically with Martinique and another thirty-two on the French West Indies that will also be of interest.

380 **Writers of the Caribbean and Central America. A bibliography.**
Compiled by M. J. Fenwick.   New York: Garland Publishing, 1992.
2 vols. 1,605p.

Fenwick's recent reference work is the most complete to-date on literature and writers of the Caribbean area. Countries are arranged alphabetically with authors listed under country of birth, under other countries of relevant residence, and by pseudonyms. Original writings are presented chronologically, followed by lists of anthologies and journals in which the author's writings appear. More than 150 Martinican writers with their work, from the 19th century to the present, are listed in some twenty pages of text.

Indexes

There follow three separate indexes: authors (personal and corporate); titles; and subjects. Title entries are italicized and refer either to the main titles, or to many of the other works cited in the annotations. The numbers refer to bibliographical entry rather than page numbers. Individual index entries are arranged in alphabetical sequence.

Index of Authors

Césaire, Aimé 274-8, 295
Césaire, Ina 348
Chamberlain, Greg 372
Charbit, Yves 174, 214, 217
Chauleau, Liliane 133, 166, 354-5, 377
Chevalier, Haakon 280
Chomereau-Lamotte, Marie 74
Clarke, Colin 178
Cohen, David W. 149
Cohen, Robin 149, 238
Colin, Patrick L. 58
Colmet-Daage, F. 16
Comitas, Lambros 371
Condon, Stephanie 182, 184
Conway, Dennis 70
Corzani, Jacques 302
Coulthard, G. R. 301
Covington, Paula H. 376
Craig, Susan 115, 266
Cross, Malcolm 180, 253
Crouse, Nellis M. 114, 140
Crusol, Jean 257-8
Cruxent, José M. 84
Cudjoe, Selwyn R. 312, 316
Curtin, Philip D. 110

D

Dash, Michael 284, 287, 306
Davies, Carole Boyce 313, 315
Davis, Gregson 277
Davis, W. M. 11, 35
Debien, Gabriel 136, 148, 150
Debretagne, L. 261
Deerr, Noel 119
Delmond, Stany 219
Dengo, Gabriel 38
Desportes, Auguste 296
Dessalles, Adrien 117
Dessalles, Pierre 159
Dessalles, Pierre-François-Régis 147
Dethan, L. 374
Diagram Group 19
Drescher, Seymour 130
Dubreuil, Guy 213
Dumoret, Marcel 23
Dupont, Louis 255
Duprat, J. P. 108
Duprey, Pierre 293
DuTertre, Jean Baptiste 118

E

Eeuwen, Daniel van 254
Egan, Cecilia M. 227
Elisabeth, Léo 149, 159
Engerman, Stanley 156
Eshleman, Clayton 274, 276, 319
Esteves, Carmen C. 294
Evans, Clifford 95
Eves, C. Washington 30

F

Fanon, Frantz 279-81
Farrugia, Laurent 225
Fenwick, M. J. 380
Fermor, Patrick Leigh 28, 282
Fido, Elaine Savory 315
Folliard, Edward T. 26
Foster, Joseph G. 286
Fournet, Jacques 63
Francis, Peter 45
Franklin, Barbara A. 286
Fraser, Linda J. 76
Freeman, Gary P. 183
Frutkin, Susan 318

G

Gaillard, Robert 283
Gallo, William K. 342
Galloway, J. H. 127
Gastmann, Albert 237, 243, 284, 375
Gautheyron, J. 16
Gauthier, Jeanne 89
Geggus, David 156
Geismar, Peter 322
Gendzier, Irene L. 323
Gilly, Adolfo 280
Gisler, Antoine 138
Glissant, Edouard 284-7, 295
Gomes, P. I. 249
Goodwin, Paul B. 237-8
Goveia, Elsa V. 160
Graham, Alan 68
Greene, Jack P. 149
Greenfield, Sidney 126
Gresle, François 200
Grieb, Kenneth J. 376
Grunevald, Henri 37
Guilbault, Jocelyne 344, 347
Gunson, Phil 372

Index of Titles

133

Index of Subjects

Demography 10, 15
  colonial 133, 157
  fertility 172-5, 186, 213-14
Departmentalization 169, 171, 231-2,
  234, 244, 246, 288
Diamant site 85, 89, 90-2, 103, 107
Dictionaries 366, 372, 375
Disease 111, 272
Dissertations 367, 373, 379
Diving, recreational 57-8
Dominica 33

E

Earthquakes 34, 39
Economy 7-8, 10, 249, 250-3
  businesses 368
  dependency on France 238-9, 240-1,
    243, 254-5
  economic development & policy 252-
    3, 257, 281
  economic patterns 70, 170, 196, 253,
    359, 367
  economic policy 257, 264, 267, 367-8
  European Economic Community 237,
    254
  export structure 269, 368
  See also History (economic)
Emigration to France 182-6
Employment in France 182, 261-2
Environmental change 13, 15, 66-7
Étages, Louis des 163
Ethnicity 208
Exports 269

F

Family 210-17
Fanon, Frantz 235, 242, 299, 301-2, 305,
  308, 312, 325-8, 378
  biographies 322-4, 325
Fauna 56, 59, 65, 76
Fish 57
Fishing 263, 341
  communities 263, 279, 339
Flora 61, 63-4, 66-9
Folklore 12, 28, 219, 339-40, 342-6, 351,
  353
Folk medicine 273, 339
Folktales 348-50, 352
Fond Brûle site 85, 90, 104

Food production 259, 266-8
Forestry 265, 271
Fort-de-France 179, 248
Freedmen 145, 149, 153, 156, 254-5, 259
French Guiana 21, 236
French Revolution 127, 147, 156, 162

G

Gardens 268-9
Geography 4, 9-10, 12-13, 15, 358
  plant 66-7
Geological history 15, 52
Geological research 40
Geology 33, 36-41, 53
Geomorphology 11-12, 35, 41, 70
Government, local 354
Glissant, Edouard 295, 299-300, 302,
  304, 307-8, 312, 329, 331-4, 376
Gravity anomalies 38, 40
Guadeloupe 16, 63, 116, 118, 124, 131,
  140, 146, 166, 169, 178, 182, 193,
  214, 236, 238, 243-7, 252, 254-5
Guidebooks 70, 72-3

H

Haiti 286
Health 272
History
  African-American 121
  British occupation 146
  demographic 111
  early colonial 114-15, 117, 122, 140,
    157, 376
  economic 116-17, 125, 135, 142-3,
    161, 251, 254, 258, 267, 375
  European interests 112-13, 123, 131,
    135, 142, 146, 168
  French in Caribbean 113-15, 122, 127,
    151, 158, 170
  general 2, 4, 8, 112-13, 118, 120, 125,
    151, 360, 364, 376
  political 116, 124, 143, 152, 167, 171,
    254, 318
  social 133, 159, 166, 333, 375, 377

I

Indians, East 27, 165, 178, 225, 229
Island arcs 38, 40, 52

138

L

Labour conditions 261-2, 269
Landforms 35, 52
Land tenure 203, 211, 269
Land use 10, 20, 66, 181, 267-9
Language 221
  French-based creole 219-20, 222,
    279
  linguistics 218, 220-1
Literature
  anthologies 293-6
  authors 369, 378
  bibliographies 308, 369, 374, 380
  children's 290
  dramas 286
  essays 284-5
  feminist 309, 313, 315-16, 369
  historical 303
  literary criticism 297-9, 300-1, 304-5,
    307, 311-12, 319, 361
  novels 282-3, 287-9, 291, 369, 376,
    380
  poetry 274, 276-8, 292-3, 295-6,
    317
  short stories 293

M

Macabou site 76, 96
Magic 340-1
Maran, René 295, 299, 302, 305, 311,
  335, 378
Marigot site 94
Marronage 148, 332
Medicine see Folk medicine
Medicinal plants 64, 273
Migration 9, 182-6
Military on Martinique 158, 162
Missionaries 25, 118, 122, 132, 137-8,
  143
Morne-Vert 201, 203-5, 207, 269
Music 342-7

N

Nationalism 124, 233, 244-5, 247
  black nationalism 235, 310, 312, 318,
    324, 326, 335
Natural history 1, 118

Negritude 277-8, 284-5, 295, 298-9,
  301-2, 306-9, 310, 313-14, 317,
  320, 329
Novels see Literature (novels)

P

Palaeontology 76
Paquemar site 83, 94, 99
Parti Progressiste Martiniquaise 233
Peasantry 115, 192, 195, 198, 201, 203,
  207, 215, 266, 281
Pelée, Mont 1, 12, 24, 33, 45-55
Periodicals 356-64
Petroglyphs 81
Pharmacopaeia 81
Physiography 11, 41, 44
Piracy 123
Plantations 126, 150, 153, 155, 192, 196,
  200, 264, 269
Plate tectonics 36, 38-9, 42, 44, 47, 52
Plays see Literature (Dramas)
Poetry 274, 276-8
Political thought 242, 275, 319, 321
Politics 7-8, 234, 366, 372
  autonomy movements 231, 246
  colonial revolts 144, 162, 164
  French policy 236-7, 239, 241, 243, 247
  workers' organizations 163
  See also Assimilation
Population 15, 50, 175, 251, 272
  African 109-10, 111, 136-7, 145,
    149-50, 176-7
  density and pressure 259
  East Indian 165, 178
  native American 132, 157, 365
  prehistorical 84, 94-6, 100-1, 107
Pottery see Archaeology (ceramics)
Poverty 209, 213
Prehistory see Archaeology

R

Racial identity 206, 280, 324
Reefs 1, 57-8, 60
Regional planning 248
Religion
  folk religion 224-8, 339
  syncretism 225, 229
  religious history 154, 223, 357
Resources, natural 259, 270

Map of Martinique

This map shows the more important towns, physical features and archaeological sites.

ATLANTIC OCEAN

La Perle

Grand Rivière

l'Anse de Belleville

Vivé

Fond Brulé

Prêcheur

Marigot

Mt Pelée 1397 m

Morne Rouge

St-Pierre

Sainte-Marie

Carbet

Morne des Esses

R. Lorrain

R. Galion

St-Joseph

Robert

Ilet Ramville

R. Lézarde

Case-Pilote

Lamentin

Fort-de-France

CARIBBEAN SEA

Baie de Fort de France

Grande Anse

Mt Vauclin

Vauclin

Diamant

Paquemar

Macabou

Rocher du Diamant

PUERTO RICO

ST. KITTS

BARBUDA

VIRGIN ISLANDS

ANTIGUA

NEVIS

MONTSERRAT

GUADELOUPE

DOMINICA

CARIBBEAN SEA

MARTINIQUE

ST. LUCIA

ST. VINCENT

GRENADA

TRINIDAD

SOUTH AMERICA

Sainte-Anne

Ilet Chevalier

Savane des Pétrifications

□● Towns linked with archaeological sites

□ Archaeological sites

Rivers

Main roads

⊕ Airport

0   5   10
          km

ALSO FROM CLIO PRESS

INTERNATIONAL ORGANIZATIONS SERIES

Each volume in the International Organizations Series is either devoted to one specific organization, or to a number of different organizations operating in a particular region, or engaged in a specific field of activity. The scope of the series is wide-ranging and includes intergovernmental organizations, international non-governmental organizations, and national bodies dealing with international issues. The series is aimed mainly at the English-speaker and each volume provides a selective, annotated, critical bibliography of the organization, or organizations, concerned. The bibliographies cover books, articles, pamphlets, directories, databases and theses and, wherever possible, attention is focused on material about the organizations rather than on the organizations' own publications. Notwithstanding this, the most important official publications, and guides to those publications, will be included. The views expressed in individual volumes, however, are not necessarily those of the publishers.

VOLUMES IN THE SERIES

1 *European Communities*, John Paxton
2 *Arab Regional Organizations*, Frank A. Clements
3 *Comecon: The Rise and Fall of an International Socialist Organization*, Jenny Brine
4 *International Monetary Fund*, Anne C. M. Salda

5 *The Commonwealth*, Patricia M. Larby and Harry Hannam
6 *The French Secret Services*, Martyn Cornick and Peter Morris
7 *Organization of African Unity*, Gordon Harris
8 *North Atlantic Treaty Organization*, Phil Williams
9 *World Bank*, Anne C. M. Salda

TITLES IN PREPARATION

British Secret Services, Philip H. J. Davies
Israeli Secret Services, Frank A. Clements

Organization of American States, David Sheinin
United Nations System, Joseph P. Baratta